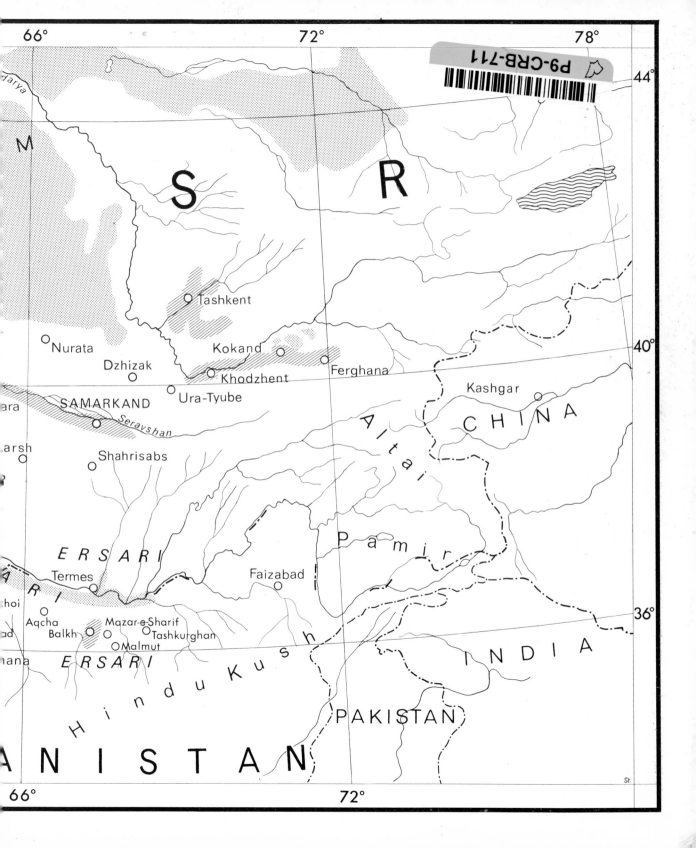

66°   72°   78°

44°

M

S   R

40°

O Nurata

O Tashkent

Kokand

Dzhizak
O
Khodzhent   O Ferghana
O Ura-Tyube

Kashgar
O
CHINA

SAMARKAND
O   Seravshan

Larsh
O

Shahrisabs
O

A l t a i

ERSARI

P a m i r

Termes   Faizabad
O

choi

Aqcha
O   Mazar-e-Sharif   36°
Balkh   O   O   Tashkurghan
O Malmut

I N D I A

hana

ERSARI

H i n d u K u s h

PAKISTAN

A N I S T A N

St.

66°   72°

Johannes Kalter

The Arts and Crafts of Turkestan

Thames and Hudson

Translated from the German *Aus Steppe und Oase: Bilder turkestanischer Kulturen* by Michael Heron

'Reflections on the Ornamentation of Central Asian Carpets': Walter Böhning
Photographs: Ursula Didoni
Documentary photographs: Museum für Völkerkunde, Vienna
Drawings and graphic design: Angela Paysan

First published in Great Britain in 1984
by Thames and Hudson Ltd, London

First published in the USA in 1984 by Thames and Hudson Inc.,
500 Fifth Avenue, New York, New York 10110

Library of Congress Catalog Card Number: 84–51235

Printed and bound in West Germany by Staib & Mayer, Stuttgart

Contents

Foreword

More than thirty years ago, I concerned myself with the early history of Central Asian mounted nomads. When I took over the Asian Department of the Linden Museum Stuttgart, I soon discovered that no more than a handful of pieces from my previous field of study existed in the collection, acquired by chance and without artistic or scholarly importance.

Financial circumstances, however, allowed very little room for manœuvre; in spite of that the first stimulus to forming an ethnographical and art collection was given.

When I decided to make a research journey to North-east Afghanistan in 1961/62, many of my colleagues asked in astonishment what a museum official who also had a large South Sea Department to take care of was looking for on the edge of the Pamirs, where 'there was virtually nothing to collect'. But a group of about 600 objects, by-products of my research trip, was assembled. A little later, it became possible to acquire the fruits of the Friedrich expedition to North-west Pakistan for the Linden Museum in an exchange deal and suddenly a collection of some 1,500 objects from the Hindu Kush region had come into being. This resulted in a rough plan for collecting, which I continued to work on systematically as from the early 70s and also collected to that end. When it became possible in 1974 to create and staff a department on the basis of the Middle East collection which already comprised 2,000 objects, I was fortunate enough to engage Dr Kalter to work with me on enlarging the department. He tackled this task with great enthusiasm and the foundations for future work were laid in the course of numerous discussions.

The Iranian territory in its broader sense and the surrounding regions to the north-east, east and south-east have become a centre of our collecting and remain one of the focal areas. On the initiative of Dr Kalter, another area was added. We collected objects from Saharan cultures and Northwest Africa so that we could represent the essentially Islamic aspects and many facets of the rural life of two clearly differentiated cultural areas inside Islam. In the process our collecting became basically directed towards planned exhibitions and was assembled piece by piece, like stones in a mosaic. Thus we approached our collecting target step by step with a relatively small number of objects.

It will be readily understood that this collecting programme had to include objects showing the way of life of a Central Asian mounted nomad culture, given the historical importance of these cultures for the whole Eurasian area. The rapid changes taking place in the way of life of present-day Turkmen make collecting difficult. Handicraft products made for personal use (knotted products, flat woven fabrics and metal work in the form of jewellery) could still be acquired comparatively easily, but the gradual disappearance of nomadic features in many sub-districts of this cultural region unfortunately meant that many characteristic features of pastoral culture can no longer or rarely be found even on the spot. We are still looking for such items in the hope of reaching the point when the culture can be adequately represented in subsequent exhibitions.

It has been a controversial point for many years whether and to what extent nomads were self-supporting in historic times, not only in regard to food, but also and above all in regard to their equipment. We will have to differentiate here between, on the one hand, the large deserts and semi-deserts of North Africa and the spacious steppes of Inner Asia and, on the other hand, areas in which land that can only be used as pasture is interspersed with oases, i. e. with arable, densely populated centres including towns. In a region like the one presented here – North-west Afghanistan, North-east Iran and Soviet Central Asia – we had to start from the fact that a symbiosis had developed, that the phenomenon of the interdependence between towns and surrounding areas which is in its specific form characteristic of great parts of the Islamic world can be observed here, too, and perhaps even better than elsewhere. It was with this concept in mind that we also collected objects from the oasis cultures, and we believe that the material in our collection which is partly presented here can prove the existence of such symbioses.

The present publication originally appeared in connection with an exhibition which was shown in Germany, Austria and Belgium. I am very happy that it has now become possible to publish an English edition, and I offer my sincere thanks to my collaborator, Dr Johannes Kalter, and to all those who helped him to present the nucleus of our collections concerning this important subject to the English speaking world. Perhaps this publication will at last stimulate one or the other scholar to take up investigations, which have been long overdue, regarding the problem of the craftmen's trade in nomadic cultures.

Friedrich Kussmaul
Director, Linden Museum
Stuttgart

Introduction

The idea of presenting symbiosis and antagonism of rural agricultural and urban cultures on the one hand and of nomadic cultures on the other hand by means of the inventory of these groups is at least ten years old. It was initiated when the author was given the task of drawing up a plan for collecting and exhibiting for the then newly founded Department of the Islamic Orient of the Linden Museum, Stuttgart.

Apart from a few exceptions, ethnologists have traditionally only dealt with rural cultures. This limitation presents no problems in the classical areas of ethnology such as Oceania or Black Africa where there are hardly any urban cultures except Nigeria. A method that achieves good results in those areas – the isolated examination of rural cultures – must inevitably lead to a distorted picture when the very advanced civilizations of the Old World are considered which are characterized by millenia-old urban cultures and an equally long exchange of peoples, ideas and products between town and country.

It may seem to a superficial observer of the history of the Islamic cultural sphere that the relationship between townsmen and nomads has always been marked by opposition. It is true that nomad armies again and again devastated flourishing cities – the town of Balkh in North Afghanistan for example has never recovered from its destruction by the troops of Chingiz-Khan in the 13th century. But it is equally true that nomad rulers who became masters of the towns which were situated in their sphere of influence gave important cultural impulses to these towns. In the 14th century, for example, Timur made Samarkand the brilliant centre of his empire which comprised nearly the whole of the East Islamic world. Under his successors, Timurid princes, Herat became the centre of one of the most important schools of book illumination in Islamic art.

We find the symbiosis between townsmen and nomads, which is so typical of the arid belt of the Old World, at the very beginning of Islamic history. Muhammad, son of a merchant from Mecca, spread his new religion, which had originated in that town, with the help of Bedouin mounted armies. Although the rapid diffusion of Islam from the extreme North-west of Africa to the Indus in less than 100 years could not have been achieved without nomad armies, Islam is ultimately an urban religion.

Because of their manifold functions, towns are focal points of cultural development in a given area. With their bazaars, they have a central economic function as the scene for business and handicrafts. Technological and stylistic innovations emerge from the bazaar. The supply of items in the bazaar (imported goods) is also a factor inducing cultural change, at least as far as it concerns material culture. Towns are religious and intellectual centres. The only way for a Muslim to acquire a traditional education was to attend a madrassah (a kind of college with boarders) in a

Ill. 1   Teke family with camels, before 1890

9

town. Towns have central administrative functions. The town bazaar is lastly the place where farmers and nomads meet to satisfy their needs for high class household goods and exchange their wares directly or through the intermediary of bazaar dealers.

Townsmen depend on this exchange with nomads. Irrigable land is much too rare and too precious to be used as pasture. The townspeople's need of animal products is covered by the exchange of goods with nomads. Traditional Islamic towns drew a considerable part of their wealth from transcontinental trade. The pack and riding animals needed for the trading caravans were provided by nomads. They also supplied the guides who led the caravans through the huge steppe and desert regions and protected them.

The relationship between townsmen and nomads could also have been exemplified with instances from North-west Africa or Arabia. Our choice fell on Turkestan for two reasons. Central Asia is a region with a very ancient urban cultural tradition. According to recent research by Soviet archaeologists, settlements of an urban type existed in Central Asia at the turn of the 4th to the 3rd millennium BC.*)

Towns such as Samarkand (Afrasiab), Bukhara and Merv were of great cultural importance when eastern Islam was at its zenith from the 9th to the 12th c., but have remained so down to the present, and were of equal importance as the better known centres of Islamic culture like Damascus, Cairo or Cordoba. Besides, Turkestan is the home of the historically most important type of nomads, the Central Asian mounted nomads, whose culture is exemplified in the present publication with material from the Turkmen.

Beside the reasons that emerge from our subject, there are others which result from the history of the collection. More than 90 % of the material published here was acquired during the past decade. Since the beginning of the 70s more and more excellent Turkmen objects appeared on the market. A great part of our collection was obtained from the trade; other objects, mainly simple tools and household goods which are essential in our attempt to present a picture of these cultures, were collected by the author during a journey to North Afghanistan undertaken in 1978 for collecting and documenting purposes. The collecting activities and the evaluation of the literature showed that there were numerous points of contact and overlappings between the Turkmen inventory and that of the rural and urban Uzbeks and Tadzhiks. We therefore deliberately collected the objects of all the groups mentioned. Our collection from the cultural spheres already mentioned comprises more than 900 objects. There are undoubtedly specialised collections (textiles and jewellery) which can offer a broader spectrum. But as we have consciously refrained from assembling similar types and from the beginning planned our collection to show not only outstanding individual pieces, but also 'cultural pictures', this relatively modest number of pieces enables us to transmit a reliable impression of the broad features of the cultures concerned. As far as we know, our collection, with its mixture of outstanding handicraft products and the simplest objects for everyday use, is the most complete outside the Eastern block.

Gathering such a collection and producing a publication like this are impossible without the help of many people. Mr Jörg Drechsel of Karlsruhe has done yeoman service in forming the collections. For his direct collaboration I should like to thank my friend Dr W. Böhning of the Völkerkunde-Museum Heidelberg who supplied the contribution 'Reflections on the ornamentation of Central Asian carpets', discussed the whole idea of the publication and checked the manuscript. I thank Mrs U. Didoni for taking the photographs. Mrs A. Paysan made the drawings and the layout and discussed questions of form and content with me. The Director, Professor Dr Kussmaul, was always ready to discuss questions of the history of the mounted nomads. Valuable ideas were provided by my colleague, Dr A. Janata, and the collector, H. Rudolph. Last, but not least I must also thank the unknown craftsmen who made these exhibits, which, as a testimony to their culture in our collection, are the best ambassadors for their peoples.

Stuttgart, July 1984   J. Kalter

---

*) 'The word town is used to describe important settlements, usually cultural, economic and administrative centres of districts and regions, whose inhabitants were mainly engaged in business and handicrafts. The ancient and medieval towns nearly always had a formidable system of fortifications.'

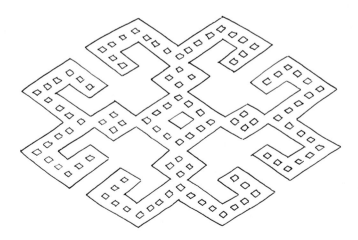

Ill. 2 Rams' horn motif on a north Afghan Kelim bag

Land and People

West Turkestan* lies in a basin at the heart of the Eurasian continent, bounded by the Caspian Sea in the west, the Kopet Dagh mountains and the Hindu Kush in the south, and the Altai chain and the foothills of the Tien Shan range in the east. There are no fixed boundaries to the north, the region of the Aral Sea. The former administrative district of Russian Turkestan with its 2.2 million square kilometres (850,000 square miles) is more than nine times the size of Great Britain.

The thousands of rivers and streams that form Turkestan's two large river systems might easily obscure the fact that the region is extremely dry. Their sources lie in the surrounding mountains which rise to a height of more than 7,000 metres. Only the two main rivers reach the Aral Sea, which, extending to *c.* 69,000 square kilometres, covers an area as large as the Republic of Ireland and is, together with the Caspian Sea (394,000 square kilometres), the remnant of a huge continental lake. The westernmost of the two rivers, the Amu Darya – the Oxus of the Ancients – has its source in the Hindu Kush and reaches the Aral Sea after about 2,500 km (the Rhine, in comparison, is *c.* 1,300 km long). The eastern river, the Syr Darya – ancient Jaxartes – rises in the mountains at the eastern edge of the basin and reaches the Aral Sea after roughly 2,200 km.

The climate at the foot of the surrounding mountains is as a rule semi-arid, with *c.* 300–400 mm of annual rainfall. Within the basin the values vary between up to 100 mm (extremely arid) and 200 mm annually (arid*). West Turkestan is part of the arid belt of the Old World, which extends from the Arabian peninsula over the Iranian Highlands as far as the Gobi. There, productive agriculture in the plains is only possible with the help of artificial irrigation, that is to say, in oases. As a glance at the map will show, the oases are situated along the rivers or at medium altitudes and in the foothills of the mountain ranges (river and foothill oases). Precipitation falls in winter and in spring. The two great rivers, fed by numerous tributaries carrying tremendous quantities of melt-water from the surrounding high mountains, reach the Aral Sea, but with a high loss of water caused by evaporation and seepage. All the region's other rivers are defeated in their fight against sand, stones, distance and the extreme summer temperatures that are characteristic of the continental climate. Before seeping away, however, they often create large oases, like the river Murghab to which the oasis of Merv owes its life, or the Zarafshan, a former tributary of the Amu Darya which now seeps away in the marshland of Bukhara.

The heart of West Turkestan (e. g., Bukhara) lies around 40° north, on about the same latitude as Madrid. The wide annual range of temperature cannot be attributed to particularly low winter temperatures; the mean temperature in January corresponds roughly to that of the Federal Republic of Germany (Trier 0.6° C, Tashkent – 1.1° C). The mean temperature in July, however, lies considerably above that of Central Europe (Trier 17.8° C, Tashkent 27.4° C, Termez 31.4° C). The differences become even more clearly visible when comparing the absolute minimum and maximum temperatures in the comparative months and stations (in °C):

	Trier	Tashkent	Termez
January			
Absolute minimum	– 20.5	– 22	– 24
Absolute maximum	13.6	28	24
July			
Absolute minimum	4.3	11	8
Absolute maximum	37.4	40	50

At Trier, the month of March has the lowest amount of precipitation (37 mm), August the highest (80 mm); the mean annual precipitation comes to 719 mm, the average duration of sunshine to 1,574 hours, with a mean relative humidity of 68 per cent in April and 90 per cent in December.

At Tashkent and Termez, the highest average precipitation falls in March (81 mm and 30 mm respectively). The months of July to September bring 3–4 mm of rainfall at Tashkent, but on average no precipitation at Termez. Tashkent has an average of 2,820 hours of sunshine; Termez, with 3,043 hours, nearly doubles Trier's total. Per annum, Trier has 163 days with more than 0.1 mm of precipitation, Tashkent has 79 days, Termez 42. These figures, viewed by themselves, provide evidence enough. Their full significance is only seen, however, when compared with the minimum

---

*) Politically, the greater part of West Turkestan now belongs to the Soviet Union; a narrow strip of land between the Amu Darya and the northern drop of the Hindu Kush is part of Afghanistan. Geographically, historically and culturally, the region is relatively coherent. The term Turkestan appeared in the 16th century and became generally accepted both in academic literature and in political terminology (Russian Turkestan + Afghan Turkestan = West Turkestan; Chinese Turkestan = East Turkestan). The name was abolished by the Soviets during the Stalin era to weaken the pan-Turkic independence movement.

*) Climates are called arid when the annual evaporation is higher than the annual rainfall. (In comparison: annual rainfall in London is around 750 mm, at high altitudes of the Swiss Alps around 3,000 mm.)

level of precipitation per annum. The figure is missing for Trier (where the average is 719 mm), but at Tashkent the minimum annual precipitation is 141 mm, at Termez 62 mm. The average precipitation per annum distorts the picture, though, in so far as precipitation is not only scarce, but also very irregular, both in its distribution through the year and in the long term. A year with plentiful precipitation may often be followed by several dry years. It is these climatic fluctuations between the years which often lead to catastrophic consequences for nomadic peoples (witness the disastrous drought in the Sahel zone at the beginning of the seventies).

Ill. 3 and 4   General view and detail of the water raising system at Bairam Ali near Merv. Photo Heger, 1890.

Ill. 5
Turkestan horse trappings. The Turkestan man's need for jewellery and display was expressed in the use of richly ornamented bridles and saddlery. These elements really need to be seen when they are in use. Se we have photographed them on suitable types of horses.

a. Head pieces, left, in the style of the Teke Turkmen, right, in the Khiva style.

b. Detail of Uzbek head piece. Ornamental neck plate, silver, fire gilded with cornelians and turquoises.

c. Detail of Turkmen head piece. Silver, fire gilded with cornelians. Dated 1274 H. = 1857 AD.

d. Detail of Turkmen head piece with mane ornamentation

e. *Saddled and bridled horses, left with Uzbek, right with Turkmen harness.*

f. *Detail of Turkmen horse décor, breast band*

g. *Detail of Uzbek horse ornamentation. Neck décor with yakhair whisk, known as a horse ornament from Soghdian times*

h. *Painted wooden saddle with bone inlays and saddlecloth with silk embroidery. 19th c, urban work*

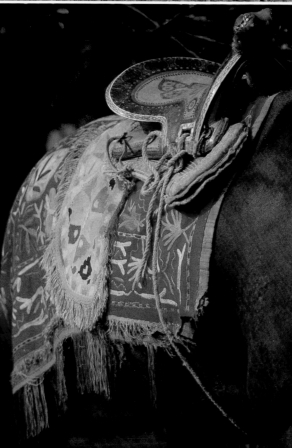

The average height above sea level of West Turkestan – the Caspian-Turanic basin – is around 50–300 m. At the western extreme on the Mangyshlak peninsula, lies the depression of Karagija, at 132 m below sea level the lowest-lying region of the Soviet Union. Large, scattered foothill and river oases are separated by vast prairies and deserts such as the Kara Kum ('Black Sand', 350,000 square kilometres) south of the Amu Darya and the Kyzyl Kum ('Red Sand', 300,000 square kilometres; the area of Great Britain, in comparison, is 230,000 square kilometres) between the Amu Darya and Syr Darya. According to Machatschek, the total expanse of irrigable land amounted to 46,000 square kilometres around 1920, that is roughly 2.3 per cent of the total area of the then Government-General of West Turkestan. During the region's heyday, in the Middle Ages, the irrigable area is said to have been two to three times larger. This seemingly low figure must not obscure the fact that individual Turkestan oases are surprisingly large in comparison with the North African oases with which the European observer is more familiar.

The expanse of irrigated land was 12,500 square kilometres in the Emirate of Bukhara – that is almost the size of Northern Ireland –, 300 square kilometres at the oasis of Khiva, and 9,200 square kilometres in the Ferghana valley – almost half the size of Wales. A glance at the map shows that, with the exception of Khiva, which is situated in the delta estuary of the Amu Darya, all the great old cultural centres from which the urban material in this book comes are foothill oases, such as Tashkent, Samarkand and Bukhara. After thousands of years of intensive cultivation, the sediments or alluvia of extremely fertile loess deposited at the foot of the mountains and along the rivers still yield adequate crops without artificial soil improvement. Adjacent to these intensively cultivated, irrigated foothill oases are other fertile regions at the edge of the mountains where agriculture (Bogara culture) yields good crops, including cereals, provided that the annual rainfall reaches 300 mm.

Irrigation of the oasis land is carried out in three ways. The most frequent is by digging. The main canal leads off from the rivers – or more usually tributaries – at an acute angle. Secondary canals then run from these at right-angles and at regular intervals, and finally the irrigation ditches are dug at right-angles again.

The second method, the so-called karez system, was developed in early Iran. Deep wells are dug at places where ground water is expected.From these wells tunnels with a gentle gradient are driven into the plain, often many kilometres long, leading the water to the oasis region where it is needed. The construction of these tunnels is only made possible by providing vertical shafts leading down to them at intervals of 20–40 m. These shafts are used for removing the excavated material, for climbing down when the canal has to be cleared of sand or pebbles, and for ventilation.

Running the canals underground reduces evaporation.

A third method is to raise the water by means of wheels with scoops, either directly operated by water power at the rivers, or driven by oxen.

The first two methods require the coordinated and prolonged effort of a comparatively large group of people for the construction and maintenance of the irrigation systems, and it may be assumed that they played a decisive role in the formation of more extensive and strictly organized communities. Correspondingly, certain oasis areas in Turkestan, such as the region around Balkh, have never recovered from the destruction of their irrigation systems following disastrous nomad invasions, particularly during the Middle Ages (Chingiz-Khan/Tamerlane). This also explains the above-mentioned two-thirds decrease in irrigable land between the Middle Ages and the turn of the century.

Considering the importance of irrigable land, it will become clear that the distribution of property was connected not to rights of land but to rights of water or irrigable land. As late as 1900, F. von Schwarz emphasized that unirrigated land had no value, whereas a hectare (about 2.5 acres) of irrigated land was worth 2,500 Reichsmarks – in a region where a 'native' could get a month's livelihood out of five Reichsmarks.

The good crops yielded by irrigable soil allow extreme population masses in a very confined space. While around 1900 the average population density of Turkestan was of the order of less than two inhabitants per square kilometre, 125,000 people lived on 85 square kilometres at the oasis of Tashkent, that is approximately 1,500 people per square kilometre. (In comparison, the average population density of Great Britain is 223 inhabitants per square kilometre).

Gardens and fields were surrounded by loam walls. Wheat was the most important species of grain that was grown. It was the staple food and occupied the predominant part of the cultivated area in the Syr Darya and Samarkand regions. Rice was grown in warm zones easy to irrigate, such as Khiva, the lower reaches of the river Zarafshan around Bukhara, and in the Ferghana Oasis. Besides the round, flat loaves made of wheat, rice was the main food of the population. Barley was chiefly used as horses' fodder. A species of sorghum which grows to a height of 4 m and has maize-like grains was cultivated as a basic food for the poor and as fodder for horses and chickens. Millet, which will grow in poor soil and with little water, played a certain role in the semi-nomads' supplementary agriculture, which was carried out with the simplest means.

Lucerne was grown as a forage plant. It yields six crops a year if properly irrigated.

The oases of Turkestan were justly famous for their first-class fruit and vegetables. The most widespread kinds of fruit were peaches and apricots. Dried, they were an essential side dish in the winter months, but also an important export article (according to Machatschek 1920: 'about 32,000 tons per annum during the past few years'). Apples and pears although grown in great quantities, were of inferior quality because the art of grafting had not been mastered. Other important types of fruit were figs, quinces, pomegranates, walnuts, almonds, pistachio nuts, and mulberries. Furthermore, mulberry trees were essential to provide food for the feeding of silkworms.

Wine growing was of considerable importance during the Middle Ages. Babur, the founder of the Moghul dynasty, who came from Ferghana and died in 1530, still enthuses about his homeland's wine in his memoirs. At that time, viticulture in Turkestan was already age-old. Arian mentions that Alexander the Great's army was supplied with wine here. Only under the fanatically orthodox Uzbek rulers did wine growing decline drastically, but it was considerably extended again after the Russian conquest. At the time of the Uzbek rulers, the cultivation of poppies for opium played an important role, but by 1900 it had completely disappeared from West Turkestan. The growing of tobacco had a long tradition, but was practised on a small scale only (v. Schwarz 1900).

Sesame, flax, hemp and sunflowers were grown for their oil. Domestic vegetables available were cucumbers, melons, rhubarb, onions and carrots.

The cultivation of cotton, which had originally been imported from India, had a centuries-old tradition, too. Cotton growing and sericulture were the foundation on which the flourishing textile workshops in the towns of Turkestan depended. Cotton has been an important export article since before the Russian conquest. As early as 1880, the longer-fibred American cotton-plant was introduced by the Russians and areas under cotton cultivation were considerably enlarged. A great number of the irrigation projects, particularly those carried out after 1920, aimed at the extension of cotton growing. Today, two-thirds of the Soviet Union's cotton harvest is gathered in the Socialist Soviet Republic of Uzbekistan. Cotton growing in Turkestan made possible the rise of Russian textile manufacture. As early as the last decades of the 19th century, cheap Russian cotton printed fabrics were beginning to supplant the products of the traditional Turkestan textile workshops more and more, bringing them almost to a standstill, except for the production of ikat materials with very simple decoration.

Wood is scarce in Turkestan, as everywhere in the arid belt. The most important species of commercial timber – used mainly for building purposes – was poplar. It is clear that, as far as vegetable products were concerned, each oasis was a self-supporting economic unit. Cattle breeding was of less importance in the oases, because of the lack of pasture land. To satisfy their need for hides, leather, wool and beef – the demand for which was small, mutton being preferred – the town dwellers found it highly advantageous to

barter their agricultural produce or domestic trade items for such goods with the nomads who exploited the steppes. Only chickens, which created no problems of space or feeding, were kept in large numbers in the oases. Cattle were used mainly as working animals for agriculture. Their meat was not appreciated, nor were milk products of any great importance in the daily diet. Animal dung was used as fertilizer or as fuel. Donkeys, or more rarely mules, mainly served as beasts of burden, but they were also used for riding by men who could not afford a horse, or by women and children. Donkeys were preferred by women, including those with wealthy husbands.

The importance attached to the breeding and keeping of horses, not only by the nomads, but also by the inhabitants of the oases, is best described in the words of F. v. Schwarz: 'Among the domestic animals kept by the sedentary population, horses play the most prominent part. There are enormous numbers of them. Every man with a claim to respectability will keep at least one horse, frequently several, and a man's financial position can be estimated with a high degree of certainty by the number and excellence of his horses.' Schwarz goes on to say that even ragged beggars often owned a horse. In addition to the undoubted desire for prestige, the particular value bestowed on horses was due to the need to move in reasonable safety and comfort through the narrow, unpaved, bustling streets of Turkestan towns without constantly getting covered with dust during the dry season or getting bogged down in ankle-deep mud after a rainstorm.

Each of these large isolated oases formed a self-contained unit and was autonomous except for the barter trade with the surrounding nomads and the long-distance trade carried on by a small number of important merchants, usually also aided by the nomads. This is why the various oases developed separate cultures, each with a character of its own. And this is why Turkestan – apart from relatively brief periods under the iron hand of great conquerors like Chingiz-Khan, Tamerlane or the first Uzbek Sheybani Khans – has never been a true political or cultural unit.

The Nomads and their Environment

As mentioned above, only 2.3 per cent of the area of Turkestan was irrigable land. We have only sporadic data about the remaining area where agriculture depended on rain, rather than on irrigation. This agriculture, the so-called Bogara culture, was restricted to a relatively narrow, cool and humid strip of the foothill zone, and was concentrated on extensive cultivation of summer corn. The yields varied considerably from year to year, though. The expanse thus used could hardly have been larger than the irrigable cultivated area, which means that approximately 95 per cent of the country's surface could – if at all – be used by nomadic cattle breeders only.

The term nomad was not introduced into academic language until the eighteenth century. Its root, let alone its definition, is a matter of dispute. As to the root, the radicals *nemos* 'pasture' or *nomos* 'rule, law' must be taken into consideration. The definition of the term nomad has led to heated discussions among historians of civilization and geographers. The present author follows the definitions of C. Rathjens (in: *Nomadismus als Entwicklungsproblem*, Bielefeld 1969). To sum up briefly what he says: 'Full nomads migrate usually in a seasonal rhythm depending on the supply of forage on the pastures (but also on the availability of water, J. K.). The entire nomadic population accompanies the herd, taking with them all their household equipment and transportable habitations, tents and yurts. They do not practise agriculture'. Full nomadism is a rare and highly specialised adaptation to extremely unfavourable areas of the earth. It may be assumed that during the past centuries this type of nomadism occured only in the large steppes and semi-steppes of the arid belt, for example with certain Tuaregs and Moorish groups of the Sahara, Arab Bedouin, Mongols, etc. The term semi-nomadism is used by Rathjens to denote a combination of pastoral (migratory) and agricultural (sedentary) ways of life and economies 'or when the tent that is used in summer is exchanged for the permanent stone or loam house in winter'. It is a characteristic feature in Turkestan that fully nomadic, semi-nomadic and sedentary groups were to be found inside the same ethnic units. In that part of West Turkestan which belongs to Afghanistan today there are still small Uzbek groups living a fully nomadic life. In the Soviet part of West Turkestan, however, the Uzbeks were part of the settled population already during the second half of the 19th century, living as farmers in villages or occasionally as artisans in the towns, and forming the ruling class with landowners, although their ancestors had conquered vast territories of West Turkestan as nomads from the 16th century

onwards. With regard to the Turkmen, we may assume that during the past few centuries subtribes were often split up into groups that lived as farmers, or as full or semi-nomads. Nomad groups might settle down when they conquered farmers' land owing to their military superiority or when they bought land after prosperous years of stock-breeding. Conversely, farmers could be forced back into the nomadic way of life as a consequence of overpopulation of farmland, destruction or decay of irrigation canals or lack of rain in agricultural areas dependent on precipitation. A fully nomadic life in the plain presupposes the possibility of relatively ample migrations. Nomads will extend their pasture areas where a political vacuum has developed or if nomads belonging to the same ethnic group form the ruling class in a centrally governed state. On the other hand, a strong central power that is ill-disposed towards the nomads may force them into unpropitious regions where they are reduced to a miserable life, with their herds diminished by fodder shortage. This, to cite but one example, was the fate of the Turkmen after the conquest of the Merv Oasis by the Russians near the end of the last century. After the Afghan-Russian border had been sealed off, pasture grounds for the Turkmen in Northern Afghanistan were so restricted that they were forced to live as semi-nomads or to settle down altogether. Another reason for nomads to settle and live as farmers was the loss of animals as a consequence of epizootic diseases.

Nomads, it is true, despise farmers, as has often been stressed. Nevertheless, this contempt kept neither groups nor individuals from settling down. Nor did farmers always remain farmers. The lives of sedentary and nomad groups, their duality and co-existence, their contacts and fights have been brilliantly described by Wolfgang König in his study of the Akhal Teke Turkmen. If the following pages take the civilization of the Turkmen as an example of a nomadic civilization, it must be admitted that this is a simplification. It seems admissible, though, because their social structure, their material culture and their cultural traditions are basically those of nomads.

To arrive at a definition of the different types of nomadism, one must consider not only the degree of sedentariness and cultivation of land, but also which animals are preferred. In Northern Afghanistan there are nomads who breed small domestic animals (Pasthtoun and Beloudch groups) besides Turkmen who are mounted nomads. West Turkestan is, like the whole of Central Asia, the classical country of the mounted nomads. F. Kussmaul has rightly said: 'The economic basis of nomads – at least of all those in the steppe belt of Eurasia – is the herd of small domestic animals, that is to say sheep and goats, cattle being of

Ill. 6 Large transport and storage bags with knotted fronts and woven backs. Above: Uzbek; below: Ersari Turkmen, northern Afghanistan. 85 by 103 cm; 99 by 148 cm

secondary importance. In comparison to these, camels and horses are not so much an economic, but rather a social and political potential' (in: *Nomadismus als Entwicklungsproblem*, Bielefeld 1969). This means that the classification is not based on the animals that are most numerous or most important to human consumption, but on those animals that enjoy the highest esteem. The horse was not the economic basis for the horse nomads nor is the camel the economic basis for Bedouin camel nomads. But horses and camels are essential as riding and above all as pack animals for the long-distance migrations of full nomads in regions with relatively poor pastures. It was their horses used as riding animals that turned peaceful herdsmen into quick and dreaded warriors who were more manœuvrable than and therefore superior to foot soldiers as well as war chariots. It was the superiority and celerity of mounted armies that made it possible to overrun the vast stretches of Inner Asia, to unite them into large nomad empires and to keep them together – if only for a short time – thanks to the possibility of swift communications. Mounted nomadism is only one and, as will be shown, a historically late form of nomadism, but historically it is no doubt the most important. These points may explain the almost incredible esteem enjoyed by horses. F. von Schwarz does certainly not exaggerate when he says: 'A Turkmen bestows his greatest care on his horse, which he loves more than wife or children, and he is more concerned for his horse's well-being than his own.' He also reports that Turkmen horses grew up in the tent together with the children, but that does not seem to have been the rule.

On the one hand, the structure and size of a herd depended on the specific needs of its owner: 'The more powerful man can keep a bigger herd because he is able to get the necessary pastures by sheer defiance and open the richest wells and the most favourable routes at the right times. His herd will show not only his economic, but to a great extent also his social and political needs and will be composed accordingly, much more so than in the case of a poor man who needs fewer riding and pack animals, but a higher proportion of live stock that yields an economic profit. In peaceful regions a group may live in scattered encampments, whereas they will if possible stay together in troubled areas so as to be better able to resist attacks' (Kussmaul 1967). The ecological factor must not be forgotten. There are great regional differences in the vegetation of Turkestan's loess and sand steppes, but it may be generally said that the most striking feature is a high percentage of species of annual grass such as aegylops; besides, there are subshrubs like wormwood (artemisia), shrubby horsetail (ephedra), bulbous and tuberous plants (tulips, different lilies, iris), a great number of different herbs (composite, labiate, and leguminous plants), thistles that grow large leaf rosettes, and others (enumeration after Volk and Machat-

schek). After the spring rainfalls the steppe rapidly turns green and is then strewn with flowers, but it dries out in May and remains brown until winter. The hot, dry summer season is not so critical for the feeding of the herds as has formerly been assumed. The vegetation dries so quickly that a kind of hay is formed on the root stocks. As a matter of fact, in certain regions of Northern Afghanistan the steppe is combed to collect hay for winter, which is the really critical season. The steppe's productivity rises again in autumn when the sheep eat the seeds of the herbs as a kind of concentrated feeding stuff. Forage may now become scarce, particularly if the herd has not been well adjusted to the available pasture area.

There is sadly little information about how much pasture ground is needed by the different kinds of animals. König says that one fat-rumped sheep, the species best adjusted to steppe pastures and therefore preferred by the Turkmen, needed 6 hectares (15 British acres) of pasture land in the region of the Akhal Teke. In Central Europe (Germany) 3 sheep are reckoned on a hectare (2.5 acres) of pasture. With regard to horses, the following calculation can be made. In Central Europe a horse needs 2 hectares (5 acres) of pasture for its self-preservation, i. e. the area needed for 6 sheep. So a horse in Turkestan would need 36 hectares (80 acres) of grazing ground. It must be considered, though, that Turkmen give their horses barley, lucerne, milk and bread as additional concentrated feeding stuff (von Schwarz; with the exception of milk, this food has to be bought by the full nomad). That means that the pasture may be somewhat smaller. Still, keeping a horse is a tremendous burden. The data concerning the required sizes of pastures will have to be considerably modified according to the situation (microclimate), the season, the specific flora, etc. – factors that really influence the quality of a pasture and the space needed by the animals. Regrettably, ethnologists and geographers have too rarely tried to collect exact data. One thing, however, is certain: to the eye of the Central European observer, the pasture areas needed are of enormous size.

From the facts given above, it will also have become clear that the nomads' live-stock is subject to heavy fluctuations. After years of above average rainfall, the herd will grow heavily, whereas lack of rain during the following spring means a drastic decrease. W. König states for the Akhal Teke Turkmen that every 4 to 5 years dry and cold winter months led to mass deaths which reduced the livestock by 30–40 per cent. Von Schwarz reports about the Kirghiz who lived under comparable conditions that 80 per cent of their stock starved to death during the unusually long and severe winter of 1859/60.

Turkmen kept horses, camels, donkeys, sheep, goats and cattle. The various species of animals were bred to satisfy various needs of their owners. This has been shown in

*Ill. 7 In the front, ceramic milk containers, with internal monchrome glaz-
ing, and gourd; behind, leather sack and stick for making butter.
Northern Afghanistan Turkmen. Heights from left right: 16.5 cm,
27.5 cm, 26 cm. Leather sack: 94 cm, stick: 118 cm*

König gives no information about the number of horses
kept. In 1911 the official estimate for the entire Government-General of West Turkestan came to a stock of
2,444,000 horses with a total population of 6,291,000. Very
probably the number of horses is much too low because the
estimate of the live-stock was used for taxation purposes. It
may be assumed that with the Turkmen the ratio of horses
per inhabitant was not much lower than the average for
Turkestan.

The percentage of camels in the live-stock of the herds
is said to have amounted to 20–40 per cent with the Turkmen, which is rather high. Camels were bred as pack animals for the Turkmen's own use and, what was more important, for trading with their settled fellow tribesmen and
the population of the large oasis regions. Camels were also
sold to caravan merchants as pack animals and to farmers
as working animals who used them for ploughing or driving
the wheels that scoped up water. They were also exported
into neighbouring Iran. Camel wool and milk, however,
seem to have been of minor importance. König has a great
number of interesting data regarding the sizes of sheep and
camel herds formed when herds of various families joined
at a feeding area around a well. The sizes varied from minimum groups to big herds. We have chosen a few examples
to indicate the spectrum:

1 family	5 members	100 sheep	15 camels
3 families	16 members	300 sheep	150 camels
3 families	15 members	60 sheep	20 camels
5 families	25 members	150 sheep	50 camels
9 families	67 members	1,500 sheep	200 camels
18 families	125 members	600 sheep	200 camels
39 families	300 members	3,000 sheep	400 camels
40 families	225 members	4,000 sheep	225 camels

To concentrate herds of that size, the supply of water
from the wells was at least as important as the supply of
food from the pastures. Some builders specialised in the
construction of wells. For building a new well, they were
given a four year-old camel or 4–5 rams.

There is yet another interesting aspect in this list. A
comparison of examples 2 and 3 or 5 and 6 will reveal that
prosperity among the Turkmen must have varied considerably. This must have expressed itself in the equipment, particularly in the quality of the men's arms, the horses' headgear and in the number and quality of the women's silver
ornaments. As the profits from stock-breeding varied and
were very uncertain, a surplus made in a prosperous year
was spent on an investment that was both stable in value
and easy to transport: it is no doubt for this reason that
more silver ornaments were hoarded by the nomads than
by the settled population.

an exemplary way by König with regard to the Akhal Teke.
As the structure of the herds differed from group to group,
we shall merely quote as examples the most relevant data
collected by König. He, too, starts his enumeration of
domestic animals with the horses, stresses the fact that
'their qualities developed by highly refined breeding gave
strong superiority in all military activities to the Teke' and
mentions that the horses were an export article much
sought after outside Central Asia, particularly in the trade
with Russia. Horses from the Akhal Teke Oasis were imported into other European states, too, and very probably
belonged to those Oriental horses that were reared in England for breeding the English thoroughbred horse (after
Glyn/Bruns: *Das grosse Buch der Pferderassen*, 3rd ed.,
Zurich 1975).

Ill. 8 Tableware and tablecloth made in Turkestan. Left: two plates with
floral décor from Khiva, 19th c. Right: plate with running glaze on yellow ground with scratched décor from Tashkurgan, 19th c. The
scratched inscription bears good wishes for the unnamed owner. Plates
with green running glaze on a yellow ground were produced in the region as from the 9th c. AD under the influence of Chinese Tang period pottery. The tablecloth is a silk ikat, of Herat manufacture, and
was acquired in Tashkurgan. D. of the plates: from 25.5 cm to 39 cm

*Ill. 9   Imported tableware and tablecloth. Exported Chinese porcelain, such
as the plate above, as used in prosperous Turkestan households
from early Islamic times. Starting in 1765, the Russian firm of Gardener made tableware with Chinese décor, as well as plates painted with
brightly coloured floral décor in the European style for the Turkestan
market. Printed fabrics the patterns of which copied the décor of the
favourite ikat cloths were made in Russian textile factories. D. of the
porcelain: from 27cm to 41 cm*

23

*Ill. 10   Apparatus for producing and finishing wool. In the background:
wooden sword and weaving frame with half-made kelim. Foreground,
from left to right: sheep-shears and container, spindle, carpet comb
and comb for cleaning wool. Northern Afghanistan.*

The backbone of a nomadic economy is sheep breeding. It is of major importance for satisfying the owner's personal need of wool as well as milk, meat and fat. W. König quotes Petrov who estimates the annual consumption of wool per economic unit (that is an extended family or tent group working jointly) at 103 kg on average.

For the tent felts alone, 128–160 kg of wool are needed. Their life lasts no more than 5–7 years, but 16–24 kg of wool are needed for repairs and the replacement of worn-out parts. Considering the large number of bags, some in pilework, others in flatweave, small rugs, ropes and other woollen items that belong to a Turkmen household, the amount of 103 kg a year seems a low estimate. According to Machatschek, a fat-rumped sheep yields 5–6 pounds of wool a year. In other words, to meet their yearly requirement of wool, a family would need to own about 33 sheep,

if one takes the highest level of productivity as a basis. This calculation shows how big a flock of sheep must be before a family can think of producing rugs for the market. Unprocessed wool was sold only by owners of large flocks. Poorer families usually processed the wool, thus trying to increase the modest surplus they had made.

For the nutrition of all Turkmen, ewe's milk was of great importance. It was either consumed while still fresh during the short milking period which began in April and lasted for 40 to 50 days. Or – more important – small, dried balls of hard cheese were made of curd cheese. They would keep for some ten months. These hard cheese balls are also known to Sahara nomads and Arab Bedouin.

Only well-to-do Turkmen could afford to slaughter sheep for their own consumption, but even they had meat only on great personal celebrations such as marriage or religious feasts such as circumcision. The recurrent yield of wool was considered more important than a single banquet. Therefore killing a healthy animal was a decision that had to be well thought out. Animals for slaughter were only disposed of in trading with the settled population to acquire goods that could not be obtained otherwise. Only rams were slaughtered. Slaughtering for the purpose of stocking supplies was done in early autumn (September/October) because then the animals were best-fed. The meat was cut into pieces and seared in the fat which was plentifully available from the animal's fat rump. The fat coated the meat, and after cooling down this coating kept off the air and thus preserved the meat for a relatively long time. A welcome, if rare, addition to the monotonous diet of rice, round flat dough-cakes and milk products (both rice and bread cereals had to be bartered) was supplied by the hunt which was carried out with dogs and hawks, and yielded hares and antelopes.

Other domestic animals kept by the Turkmen were goats, donkeys and cattle. Goats were kept in small numbers among the flocks of sheep and contributed in a modest way to the meat and milk supply. Donkeys were sometimes used as pack animals by poorer people. It may be assumed that cattle, used as working animals, only played a role with the semi-settled or settled population. It is true that in summer the herds in the Kara Kum Desert never moved more than 8–25 km away from the well (W. König), which is a distance that can be covered by a herd of cattle. But with the brooding summer heat one always had to be prepared for a well that was no longer rich enough for the whole herd or that had dried up altogether. In some cases wells were 35–70 km apart – a distance that can only be covered by sheep. In other cases the distances amounted to 150–170 km; without risking losses, these can only be overcome with camels. What makes cattle raising impractical for nomads is not only the poorness of the pastures, but the fact that cattle need much more forage than camels, sheep, goats, or donkeys. With the help of camels, a certain amount of water and if necessary concentrated food stuff can be carried along for the few riding horses of a nomad group, but this cannot be done for a cattle herd.*

The reader may have been surprised at the breadth of this introduction to the physical and human geography of West Turkestan. There are few regions on the earth where the growth of a civilization depends so much on the geographical conditions as in the arid belt of the Old World. It has therefore seemed essential to put together and impart to the reader the relevant facts – no doubt still too short for some specialists interested in particular problems. Certain simplifications were inevitable. As a standard work, Machatschek's *Landeskunde* can still be recommended. He is a child of his times in his remarks about the population of Turkestan, but as far as the compilation and interpretation of geographical facts are concerned, his work is indispensable.

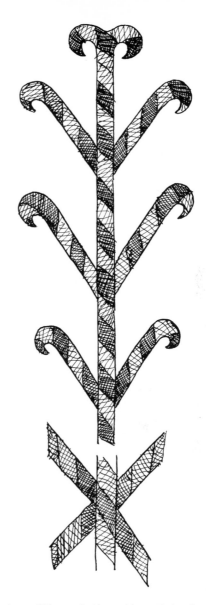

Ill. 11 Stylised tree of life topped with rams' horns. Embroidered motif from a Turkmen woman's cap.

*) Karakul sheep, whose fleeces are an important export article today for Afghanistan and the Socialist Republic of Turkmenistan (Persian lamb or Astrakhan), cannot be kept under the conditions of the nomadic pastoral economy. Although a great number of Turkmen herdsmen working stationarily make their living out of Karakul breeding – between 1955 and 1969, 2.8–6.5 million Karakul sheep yearly were counted in North Afghanistan – this modern development geared to market requirements is beyond the scope of this book. For the year 1920, Machatschek gives an export rate of 400,000 fleeces a year for Russian Turkestan.

The Peoples of Turkestan

More than a dozen important peoples and groups of tribes live in Turkestan, but only three of them deserve special attention in our context: the Turkmen, the Uzbeks, and the Tadzhiks. Their respective living spaces – the steppes, foothill and river oases – and the ways in which these are exploited have been described in the geographic introduction. This chapter will be followed by a survey of the long and eventful history of Turkestan. The following chapter about settlements and dwellings will provide an introduction to the main section of this book – the material culture. We will therefore confine ourselves here to essential background information on languages, demography, distribution of the settlement areas, economy, and cultural change of the three peoples mentioned above.

The Turkmen

Inside Turkestan, the Turkmen have always had a special position. Their dialect belongs to the Oghuz – the West Turkic – group of languages related to the Ottoman language. Most other Turkic peoples living in Turkestan speak East Turkic languages. The ancestors of the Turkmen of today invaded the region east of the Caspian Sea, advancing through Turkestan from the east, at the end of the 10th and the beginning of the 11th centuries, as a part of the Oghuz. Until the beginning of the 16th century, they had a part in the foundation of various Turkish-Islamic empires (Seljuks, Kara and Ak Qoyoulus). Since then they have been living as stockbreeders (nomads or semi-nomads) or as sedentary farmers, having no more political importance, but being an element of constant disturbance for their sedentary neighbours in Iran, the Khanate of Khiva, and also the Emirate of Bukhara. According to von Schwarz and Vambéry, their much-dreaded alaman-raids which yielded not only the animals and valuables of the assaulted, but also, as their most important booty, slaves, had become a more profitable source of livelihood during the 19th century than the yield provided by agriculture. In the frontier areas of North-East Iran alone, the Turkmen are supposed to have captured a million slaves during the 19th century.

The Iranian emperors again and again sent punitive expeditions against them. They frequently suffered devastating defeats, but contributed to a shifting of the pasture and settlement areas of Turkmen subtribes. Thus, since the 16th century, certain subtribes dissolved or were incorporated into neighbouring Turkmen groups, whereas others, such as the Teke, gained in significance. In their campaigns to conquer Turkestan the Russians suffered their heaviest losses in 1879 while trying to take the Turkmen fortress of Dengil or Geok Tepe. Of the 3,000 Russian soldiers who participated in this futile assault, 200 were killed and more than 250 were wounded. For this defeat, the Russians took a dreadful revenge. After the conquest of Dengil Tepe, in 1881, 6,500 Turkmen lay dead. This defeat marked the end of Turkmen resistance to the Russian conquest. Another reason that led to shifts within the structure of tribal organization were armed conflicts between Turkmen groups themselves. A glance at the historical survey in König's *Achal Teke* will show how complex these events were. The 24 Turkmen subtribes which have been maintained since the 11th century have not been substantiated by ethonological research up to now. For our purposes here, only four are of major importance: the Teke, who are responsible for the majority of the silver ornaments, as well as a few textiles and knotted fabrics presented in this book; the Yomut represented by their highly individual ornaments and again by textiles; the Ersari from whom come most of our household effects; and, to a certain degree, the Saryk. The greatest part of the items illustrated here were made during the last decades of the 19th and the first two decades of the 20th centuries. The market-orientated production of carpets and the breeding of Karakul sheep, which have led to considerable changes in the economic structure and consequently in Turkmen civilization as a whole, commenced on a larger scale only after that period, and can therefore be excluded from this work.

The total number of Turkmen today is estimated at approximately 1.9 million. In 1911, Machatschek reckoned the number of Turkmen living in the Government General of Turkestan (i. e. exclusive of the Iranian and Afghan regions) at 480,000; today 1.5 million live in the South of the Soviet Union, mainly in the SSR of Turkmenistan. The group most imortant to us are the Teke. About 400,000 Turkmen are settled in North Afghanistan along the Afghan-Soviet frontier, the main area stretching from the north of Mazar-e-Sharif to the mouth of the river Murghab. Most of them belong to the Ersari tribe, but there are also Saryk and a few Teke families who for the most part only arrived after 1920 as refugees from the Soviet Union. Some 20,000 Turkmen live in North-West Iran near the coast of the Caspian Sea, with Gonbad-e-Qabus as their centre; most of them belong to the Yomut tribe. Small groups of Turkmen who remained in Turkey, Iraq and Syria have been almost completely assimilated.

Concerning Turkmen cultural change, little can be said with certainty about changes in the material culture due to reasons other than the above-mentioned changes in the economic basis. The possessions of agricultural groups are bound to be different from those of nomadic groups. Items which can be proved to be older than 100 to 150 years are extremely rare. Among all the peoples in this region, a conspicuous decline in handicraft skills can be observed.

Although the forms and ornamentation remain unchanged, the pieces and their décor become coarser, and there is a tendency towards increasing their size. With later pieces, the clear ornament that can be grasped at a glance tends to be blurred. With silver ornaments, for example, it is often no longer possible to decide with certainty whether the décor consists of the gilded areas or those left with a silver surface – we will point out such examples. On the whole, we think that there is enough evidence to believe that the possessions of the nomadic Turkmen have not undergone any essential changes since they migrated into the steppe regions of Turkestan serveral hundred years ago. Turkmen ornamentation is based on (probably) Turkic steppe and early Islamic traditions. The obvious relationships to East Asian, Indian, and post-early-Islamic Iranian ornamental traditions, which are so typical of urban Turkestan material, are lacking. Owing to the relative isolation in which nomads live, their possessions and stock of ornaments are probably always more independent of fashions and trends than those of urban population groups. It is certainly correct to say that Turkmen civilization is characterized by a great respect for tradition.

For centuries, the Yomut were, more than any other Turkmen group, exposed to Iranian influence. We may assume that the particular forms of jewellery and ornamenta-

Ill. 13   Tree of life abstracted to a flowering shrub. Embroidered motif on a man's cap from Bukhara.

tion they developed were, to a large extent, created under that influence.

The Uzbeks

The ancestors of the Uzbeks had, like those of the Turkmen, invaded Turkestan as armed nomads. The name of this people, speaking an East Turkic dialect, possibly goes back to one of the leaders of the Golden Horde of the Mongols, Uzbek Khan (1312/13–1340). The process of the formation of the Uzbek people was extremely complex, again like that of the Turkmen. It was brought about in the 15th century when Turkic, Mongol and old-established Iranian groups fused during the decay of the Golden Horde. In the 16th century, part of the Uzbeks conquered the most important Turkestan towns and established themselves there, forming the leading class with considerable contingents of urban merchants and – to a lesser extent – artisans. Others settled down as farmers in the villages of the oases. In Russian Turkestan, the Uzbeks had abandoned the nomadic way of life almost completely by the 19th century, but small nomad Uzbek groups did exist in North Afghanistan until very recently. The total number of Uzbeks is estimated at approximately 11 million today. About 9 million of them live in the South of the Soviet Union – 7.7 million in the Uzbek SSR, the remainder is scattered amongst the other Central Asian Soviet republics. In 1911, Machatschek states that the number of Uzbeks living in the Government General of Turkestan amounted to about 1.83 million. The settlement area of the Uzbeks in North Afghanistan is scattered from Maimana in the west to Faizabad in the east. In North Afghanistan, too, most Uzbeks live as merchants and artisans in the towns.

Uzbek tribal structure lost its importance during the past century owing to the sedentary, mostly urban way of life. The Uzbeks splintered early into a great many small states independent of each other, which is why their civilization is characterized not by tribal, but by regional differences (Uzbeks of Khiva, Uzbeks of Bukhara, etc.).

Ill. 12   Trefoil motif from 12th-c. relief on a Ghaznevid gravestone and above from a piece of 19th-c. Ersari jewellery.

Ill. 14   Turkestan metal vessels: left: sherbet bowl, copper with floral and written décor, 16th or 17th c. The piece was later also used as a cooking pot; right: pouring vessel, tinned copper with engraved floral and geometric décor, 19th c., in a form which is already proved in pre-Christian times. Both from Bukhara. H. 20.5 cm, d. 30 cm; h. 12 cm, length with beak 31.5 cm

We will deal with their material culture after introducing the Tadzhiks, since the culture of the Uzbeks cannot be separated from that of the Tadzhiks.

The Tadzhiks

In the early Middle Ages, the word 'tazi' was the Iranian term for Arabs, that is to say Muslims. It was then used by the Turkic invaders who had not yet been converted to Islam to denote those – mainly Iranian – groups living in Turkestan who had been islamized at a very early period. Today the name 'Tadzhik' is a collective term which includes all those population groups in Turkestan and Afghanistan that speak a West Iranian dialect closely related to modern Persian. Nomad Saka and Massagetae as well as the inhabitants of the twons – Soghdians, Khorezmians, and Bactrians – were involved in the formation of this language and population group; the term 'tribe' seems even more problematic here than when applied to the other population groups of Turkestan. The Samanid empire which flourished during the 9th and 10th centuries (the first 'Iranian' foundation of a state after Islam took over, cf. chapter on history page 36) and which was of great importance for further cultural development, is considered as Tadzhik. About 2.7 million Tadzhiks live in the Soviet Union today, the greatest part in the SSR of Tadzhikistan, roughly 650,000 in Uzbekistan. Janata (1981) estimates the number of Tadzhiks in Afghanistan at 3.6 million (which would make them the second biggest population group of that country after the Pashtouns). One has to distinguish between the mountain Tadzhiks and the Tadzhiks of the plain.

In our context, the Tadzhiks of the plain are more interesting, particularly in that part of Turkestan which belongs to the Soviet Union today. There, they live as farmers, but they also form a considerable part of the population of the towns where they are mainly engaged in trade and business.

Since the 16th century, the urban civilizations of Turkestan have been supported chiefly by Uzbeks and Tadzhiks together. The civilization of the cities emerged from a combination of Iranian and Turkic cultural elements which were moulded according to Islamic conceptions; as has already been mentioned, decisive impulses were given during the Timurid period. Ideas were also received from Persians, Afghans, Indians, Chinese and others who were living in Turkestan towns as merchants, and by means of the trade effected with their countries of origin which at times was very busy. The material culture of the Turkmen is a culture shared by that particular people, whereas the culture of the cities of Turkestan is a mixture of cultures in which the above-mentioned peoples have a share, but also other peoples living in the melting-pot of those cities. We know, for example, that a considerable number of the textile artisans were Jews. Although material published by the Israel Museum of Jerusalem seems to indicate that the Jews were completely assimilated, with the exception of their own script and the production of ritual objects, it cannot be excluded that Jewish cultural heritage contributed to the material culture of Turkestan cities.

If today Arabs are only to be found in one of the smaller settlements on the Amu Darya as compact groups, it may nevertheless be assumed that they, too, exerted a certain influence on the development of Turkestan's material culture. This also applies to the great nomad peoples of the Kazakhs and Kirghiz who must however be excluded from this publication since their possessions are not represented in our collections.

Travellers and scholars of the past centuries were per-

Ill. 15 Cast iron pots; the two on the left imported from Russia, the right-hand one with rough seams is a north Afghan product. D. from left to right: 36 cm, 22 cm, 27 cm

plexed by the extreme variety of the ethnic, linguistic and cultural picture offered by Turkestan cities. In the reports of the past century, and still by Machatschek, the old established Iranian (e. g. Tadzhik) Turkestan town dwellers who had adopted the Turkic language were referred to as 'Sarts'. The same name was given to Kirghiz and Kazakh nomads who had settled down in towns. The confusion of terms is well described by von Schwarz: '. . . With regard to the term Sart, such a confusion had arisen that I often felt quite dizzy when I read what different travellers had written about Sarts, Tadzhiks and Uzbeks, so that I was sometimes unable to find out whether what a given author said referred to the Sarts, the Tadzhiks, or the Uzbeks – although I spent fifteen years of my life amongst those peoples.' Consequently, in more recent studies, the term Sart has been abandoned. In older works, most artisans as well as the greater part of those who make use of the artisans' products are called Sarts, too (in the photographs and other illustrations). Therefore the only possible procedure is to ascribe the material culture of Turkestan towns globally to a particular town or region. Whether a ewer, a waterpipe, a piece of jewellery, etc. originates from Khiva or Bukhara can be made out in many cases; the question to which ethnic group the artisan who made a given object and to which ethnic group its buyer belonged must remain undecided.

The possessions of an urban household during the last third of the 19th and the first decades of the 20th century – the period we are dealing with – consisted of three components:

1. Objects produced in people's own homes or by the extended family for their personal needs. The best-known products of that category are susanis (needlework), that is to say embroidered curtains for niches, wall drapings, bed-spreads, prayer cloths, etc. To my knowledge, they are not ascribed to particular ethnic groups, but are differentiated according to local styles (Bukhara, Nurata, Samarkand, Tashkent).

2. Local bazaar production. The bazaars of Turkestan cities had a certain catchment area which, as far as luxuries and semi-luxuries like jewellery or high-quality metalwork was concerned, must have corresponded to the territory of the respective khanate (Khiva, Bukhara, etc.).

3. Imported goods. Imported goods have always played a part in cities with strong foreign trade connections. There is evidence that Chinese porcelain was used in upperclass households even in the 19th century. From 1765 on, Chinese porcelain as well as local ceramics were more and more replaced by items manufactured in Russia (Gardener, and other makes). Among textiles, it is remarkable that the use of brocade was always important. As far as we know, brocades were, however, never produced in Turkestan cities. When comparing items that can be proved to originate from Turkestan cities with others known to us, it can be concluded that they were imported most probably from India, partly perhaps also from Iran. What was more important to and more fateful for the artisans in the town bazaars was the influx of cheap Russian printed cloths (mostly large flower designs in bright colours, but also printed copies of ikat patterns, cf. Ill. 9) – a development that must already have begun in the late 19th century.

The simpler household objects like jugs and cooking pots, normally of tinned copper, were replaced by cast iron items imported from Russia.

This process of cultural change and innovation which started in the bazaars must by no means be underestimated. Certain items of personal possessions became more or less uniform throughout Turkestan. Imported goods were integrated into the existing civilization to such a degree that it would not be justifiable to overlook that material in our

29

Ill. 16   Pot Salesmen, Bukhara, before 1890

attempt to describe Turkestan's traditional civilization. It cannot escape the observer's notice, though, that cheap European imports entering into competition with the local trade led to its rapid decay. Machatschek says as early as 1920 that 'the importation of cheap Russian mass products resulted first in a quantitative, but soon after also in a qualitative decrease of the local trade. It degenerated into a skill which was practised solely to make money easily and quickly. Artisans tried to copy the inferior European products, introduced European patterns, colours and machines, and ended up by losing all connection with Art.'

The threefold division of towndwellers' possessions described above is also applicable to nomads, with certain modifications; these will be illustrated later by means of selected examples.

The reader may expect from this description of a few of the peoples that live in Turkestan to find an immense variety and great dissimilarities in the cultures of the Turkestan peoples. These do exist, but they are reduced by the unifying bond that binds them all: Sunnite Islam.

Bukhara and Samarkand were cities to equal other centres of the Islamic world like Cairo, Baghdad, or Isfahan. They belonged to the most important cultural centres of the Islamic World. Data given by Pander produce evidence for this. Around the turn of the century, there were 13,144 mosques in the Government General of Turkestan of which 1,200 were Friday mosques (comparable in importance to Christian cathedrals), that is to say there was one mosque for every 700 believers. 'Around the turn of the century, 103 madrassas are said to have existed in Bukhara. . . They were attended by some 10,000 students educated by about 1,000 teachers.' Islam played a part in the rise to greatness of Turkestan cities. The narrow-mindedness and fanaticism of Islamic mullahs isolated on the outermost edges of the Islamic world contributed to the decline of these cities. The nomads' conversion to Islam was relatively superficial. In their religious practices, their belief in amulets and their ornamentation one always has to reckon with the survival of pre-Islamic, shamanistic ideas. The number and the variety of forms of the amulets show how much the nomads' popular religion differs from the concepts of orthodox Islamic theology.

Historical Survey

The historical role of that region has rarely been more aptly described than with these words: 'As the heart of the Eurasian continent, central Asia (author's note: and West Turkestan as part of Central Asia) had two particular, contradictory functions in history. On the one side, its immense extent, predominant dryness and want of natural connecting roads had the effect of keeping apart the civilizations at its periphery. On the other hand – and this is its most positive contribution to the dissemination of civilization – it formed a narrow, but almost continuous connecting road between these same civilizations. This function arose from its central location. Central Asia presented itself not only as an ideal territory for people's migrations, but also as an axis for the great trade routes; it was of essential importance to Chinese silk trade with the West.' (Hambly). This statement certainly astonishes those readers who have obtained their idea of Central Asia, of Turkestan from the reports of European 19th century travellers. Since the first travelogues appeared in the past century, one has been accustomed to seeing Turkestan as a country on the periphery, in a dead area of the world's history. However, this is a late historical development. During the longest period in its history which we can consider Turkestan was a country situated in the centre, a country that was traversed by peoples, merchants, and armies. This undoubtedly brought a lot of unrest and suffering, but also long periods of affluence and brilliant culture.

Russian archeologists date the first evidences of man to the Paleolithic. Neolithic settlement areas were discovered in the Karatau Mountains (east of the Syr Darya river), rock paintings dating from the same period were found near Termez. The first proofs of the transition from the civilizations of hunters and gatherers to those of settled farmers and stockbreeders, dating from the 6th millenium B.C., were discovered in the South of Turkmenia; incidentally, already allied to signs of simple irrigation methods. Around 5000 B.C. appeared th first painted pottery ware, made without a potter's wheel. The use of implements made of copper dates back to 4000 B.C.

The early development of urban civilizations – at the turn of the 4th to the 3rd millenium – has already been mentioned in the Introduction. The results of excavations undertaken at Altyn Tepe (near the Iranian frontier) and other sites show that towns of the same type as the Ancient Oriental towns sprang up and that they were in constant touch with Mesopotamia and, from the 3rd millenium on, with the Indus valley and its civilization. These urban civilizations die in the middle of the 2nd millenium B.C.

Later, at the beginning of the 1st millenium B.C., towns emerge again in the sphere of the subsequent Graeco-Bactrian empire the centre of which was in present-day north Afghanistan. It may be assumed that the founders of those towns were East Iranian groups who had invaded that region by means of war chariots; they were part of the great Indo-Iranian immigration wave.

Vast areas of Turkestan emerged into the light of history when they became the eastern provinces of the Achaemenid Empire, which had been founded by Cyrus the Great in 550 B.C. after his victory over the Medes. His empire had its centre in the Persis, part of the central region of present-day Iran. Cyrus himself had already tried to extend his influence to Central Asia, and was killed during a battle against the Massagetae (warlike mounted warriors who will be dealt with below) on the Jaxartes (Syr Darya). Darius succeeded finally in securing the eastern provinces permanently for the Achaemenid Empire. According to Herodotus, the eastern provinces paid extensive tributes in the form of gold, silver, lapis lazuli, and turquoise, mainly for the adornment of the residences of Persepolis and Susa. The irrigation systems in the oasis regions were considerably expanded. The first reliably determined war between peoples of the Iranian and Turanian regions was followed by 200 years of fruitful cooperation of the greatest importance to the further development of civilization in Turkestan.Zoroaster, the founder of the dualistic state religion of Ancient Iran, came from Bactria; he was born probably around the end of the 7th century B.C.

Alexander the Great's troops put a sudden end to the Achaemenid Empire in 330 B. C.: In 329 they conquered the Soghdian capital Marakanda (the Samarkand of today), and by 326 Transoxania was incorporated into the Greek sphere of influence. For military protection of the conquered regions, a number of towns were founded, e. g. the Herat of today, in which Alexander left Macedonian veterans who were to serve as garrison troups. Alexander's marriage with Roxana, a daughter of the Soghdian ruler, secured the conquest politically. After the early death of Alexander the Great in 323 B.C., the part of his empire that concerns us fell to his general Seleucos, founder of the Seleucid dynasty. As most rulers of that dynasty neglected the Eastern provinces, the Seleucid governor of Bactria refused his masters further obedience in 239 B.C., founding the Graeco-Bactrian Empire which survived for a hundred years, with Bactra (present-day Balkh in North Afghanistan) as its capital.

Nisa, situated near the present city of Ashkhabad, and

other important towns in the regions bordering on Bactria to the west belonged to the empire of the Parthians, a warlike people of mounted nomads who ruled over Iran and, in subsequent centuries, parts of Mesopotamia. After the founder of that dynasty, Arsaces, it was called the Arsacid Empire.

This circumstance directs our attention to the development of the steppes. So far, only towns situated in oasis regions have been mentioned in this historical introduction. How were the steppes exploited? Scholars (Jettmar, Kussmaul) now assume that farmers had moved their settlements forward into the arid steppes along the rivers. This process may have been stimulated by the fact that – according to the results of recent Soviet investigations – the steppe limit moved 400 km to the north during the second half of the 1st millennium, under the influence of extreme aridity and heat. An important factor in the economy of the steppe farmers was no doubt stock and horse breeding, which, after the climatic shift, might have gained in significance. It is conceivable that a division of labour developed between farmers and (dependent or related) herdsmen. It is not known when pastoral nomadism came into being as an independent economic system. Nor is it known where this system originated, although many facts point to North-West India. The formation of pastoral nomadism was of great importance to the exploitation of the arid regions; historically, it is only of minor interest. Another development which had its rise outside Turkestan was to gain an importance for the whole of Eurasia which cannot be overestimated and which influenced the destiny of vast parts of Asia and often – directly or indirectly – of Europe for more than 2,000 years:

The development and significance of mounted nomadism.* As is proven by finds of large quantities of bone fragments at sites used by Neanderthal and Cro-Magnon Man, wild horses were favourite game animals of prehistoric hunters. The domestication of the horse seems to have taken place in the Ukrainian steppes in the 4th millennium B.C. At first, horses were kept as animals for slaughter, but they may also have been used as pack animals. In Mesopotamia, onagers, a kind of donkey, had been used as draught animals as early as the 3rd millennium B.C. In the 2nd millennium, onagers were replaced by horses. After the invention of the light spoked wheel around 1700 B.C., rapid war chariots contributed to a decisive change of military technique, which can best be compared to the introduction of tanks in World War I.

It is not known when and where horses were first used as riding animals. The forms of snaffles and bits which were spread throughout the Eurasian steppes by the first

nomads are similar to those known in the Caucasus Mountains and South-East Europe (the Pontic region) in pre-nomadic times. Thus the first use of mounted warriors took place in the West (auxiliary Hittite troops in the battle near Kadesh in 1268 B.C.). In this region we also find the first horse-riding people about whom written sources exist, the (Thracian) Cimmerians, shortly after the turn of the 2nd to the 1st millennium B.C. At about 700 B.C., they are driven out by the first mounted nomad people whose name is known to us (from Herodotus), the Scythians, who are supposed to have come from the Volga basin. It seems that the use of horses in battle and mounted nomadism emerged more or less simultaneously. Just as the first use of cavalry is shown to have occurred in the West, the first mounted nomads also seem to have come from the West. Kussmaul has very convincingly pointed out that the interpretation of archaeological excavations is extremely difficult: 'tombs of horsemen need not be tombs of nomads (just as statues of riders are not monuments to nomads), as one may all too quickly be inclined to assume, especially when interpreting findings for which – with regard to historical period and cultural environment – the one or the other explanation might be correct.'

To sum up, it can be said that mounted nomadism must have originated in the 9th century B.C. This new cultural feature spread with breathtaking speed. 'In the course of the 8th and 7th centuries, an empire had come into being in the north of Central Asia which was unique, stretching as it did from east Turkestan over the Aral and the Caspian Sea and well into Europe: the empire of the Saka.' (Pander). Another important group of nomads, the Massagetae, possibly just a subgroup of the Saka, had their sphere of influence to the west of Lake Balkhash. Representations of Saka, delivering tribute, can be seen on reliefs at the staircase to the audience hall (the adanapa) of the Achaemenid Kings at Persepolis. It was the Saka and Massagetae who offered the fiercest resistance to Alexander the Great during his conquest of Turkestan.

Apart from the speed with which this type of nomadism spread, one phenomenon is particularly astonishing. Already in the 5th century B.C., nomads on horseback appear in an outfit that will not change during the two millenniums to come, except for a few minute variations. Costume and weapons of the mounted warriors were adapted to the new requirements. Trousers replaced voluminous, toga-like garments, boots took the place of the usual light footwear. A pair of trousers very wide at the waist and just covering the knees, found in a Hunnish tomb which was dated to the 2nd century, is of a cut that is still customary in the Orient today (Trippet). The mounted nomad warriors' most important and – till firearms came into use – most dreaded weapon was 'the short reflexive bow worn in a case called gory attached to the belt, and the short sword,

---

*) This exposition is mainly based on the publications of Jettmar, Kussmaul and Trippett.

the akinakes, attached in a similar way, and easy to handle.' (Jettmar 1966). From the 5th/6th century A.D. on, the short sword was superseded by the sabre, which has remained the classic horseman's weapon up to the present. The saddles used today were developed from felt and fur covers (Ill. 5). Very simple early types – two leather cushions sewn together lengthwise and filled with horsehair, with two curved wooden connecting pieces at the front and the back – were found in princes' tombs in the Altai Mountains, which date back to the 6th to 3rd centuries B.C. The type of saddle that has been in use in Iran and Central Asia up to the present time was fully developed by 1300 A.D. The creation of another innovation important to riding peoples – stirrups – has not yet been completely clarified. At any rate, in the 5th century A.D., they had spread at least throughout the whole of Central Asia.

The expansion of mounted nomadism is historically no doubt the most important process that began in Central Asia. Without the wavelike migrations of warlike peoples on horseback there would have been no incursions of the Huns in Central and Western Europe (Battle on the Catalaunian Plains against Attila, 451 A.D.) and of the Goths in Italy and Spain. Without the migrations of the Avars who thrust forward from North Turkestan to Eastern Europe and who were ruling the Hungarian steppes around 560, there would have been no Great Bulgarian Empire. (It was probably the Avars who introduced sabres and stirrups into Europe; Hambly 1969). Without the conquest of a great empire by Turkic nomads there would have been no Turks besieging Vienna (last in 1683). A development that started in the expanses of the Asian steppes some 3,000 years ago influenced the history of Europe till well into modern times.

For Turkestan, the emergence of mounted nomadism marked the beginning of an era which lasted until the 19th century and which was characterized by the constant conflict between the sedentary population and the nomads, the age-old fight – and often hate – between Cain and Abel; but also by symbiotic forms of coexistence. To develop fully, the steppes as well as the oases depend on peaceful exchange. Ferdinand stresses the fact that nomads are more dependent on the settled population: 'This fact (author's note: the proximity of the nomads' living-space to that of the sedentary population) has led to a specialization which has made the nomad more dependent on contact with farmers, artisans and merchants than vice-versa. The nomads cannot keep up their particular way of life without agricultural products such as wheat and corn, which constitute their main food – bread.' This statement is correct when applied to the present; with regard to the past, it is rather doubtful. If need be, nomads were able to live on their herds, whereas towns declined and decayed when they were cut off from their trade routes by nomad groups disturbing

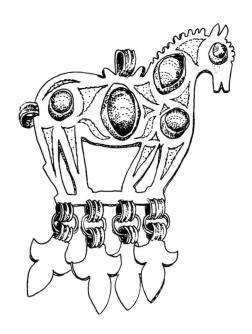

Ill. 17 Horse-shaped Teke Turkmen ornamental pendant

the peace. For this reason and although it seems to have been desirable for reasons of state to make them sedentary – nomads often managed to evade governmental control – they have often been assigned the role of the villains in historiography. We will show that Turkestan experienced the most brilliant periods of its history under nomadic rule.

After this excursion into the development and importance of mounted nomadism the further history of Turkestan will only be delineated in rough outline, and a more exhaustive description will only be given where it seems essential to the comprehension of our subject. We will have to direct our attention mainly to five points: the Turkic penetration of the region, the Islamic conquest, the Mongol empire of Chingiz-Khan and his successors, the empire of Timur and the Timurids, and, finally, the last unification of Turkestan under the Uzbek Sheybanid Khans and its subsequent splitting-up into khanates mostly governed by Uzbek rulers.

But let us take up the thread again. Parthians, warlike mounted nomads, had conquered the western regions of Turkestan around 250 B.C. The Graeco-Bactrian Empire which had its centre in the Northern Afghanistan of today could survive a hundred years longer.

Nomad incursions from the East sealed the fate of the Bactrian Empire around 140 B.C. The Sakas who came from the northern parts of Central Asia won a huge empire which stretched from North Afghanistan to India. The first ruler of this Indo-Bactrian Empire to be attested on coins resided at Taxila. From 129 B.C. on, the Parthian Empire also suffered from incursions by the Saka nomads. The last century B.C. may be called the century of the Sakas. Turkestan was divided amongst five Saka family groups. The leader of one of these groups became the founder of the Kushan Empire the centre of which was in North India. In our context it is important to note that Buddhism expanded into Turkestan during that period and that trade on the Silk Routes was booming. Essentially, there were three routes. One led from Tunhuang via Karashar (from where a branch went to Turfan – Kokand – Bukhara – Merv) to the Gulf region. The second went from Karashar to Kashgar – Tashkurgan – Bactra etc. The southern route led from Kushung to Tshaklyk – Khotan – Tashkurgan. In return, goods like woollen tapestries, gems, metalware, and especially Alexandrian glass were imported from the Roman Empire. Next to the Roman and the Parthian Empires the Kushan Empire was the most important centre of power of its time, and via the latter open to intensive influences from the west. Of greater importance to the development of art and civilization of Turkestan than these western influences was no doubt the first intensive cultural contact with India – a contact that has never been completely interrupted since that time, but which is often neglected by scholars who emphasize the more obvious connections with China and Iran.

Probably weakened by a disastrous smallpox epidemic (Hambly 1966) which spread along the trade routes as far as South Arabia, the Kushan Empire collapsed under the attack of nomads from the North and of troups of the new great power in the West, Sassanian Iran. Ardashir I, the founder of the dynasty, defeated the last of the Parthian rulers in 224 B.C.; already by 227, the Kushan King surrendered. Turkestan was divided into Iranian provinces, with the exception of Khorezm, whose rulers remained independent until the middle of the 5th century A.D. The subsequent rule of a Hunnish group, the Hephtalites, which lasted one hundred years, has left few traces in the country; culturally, it was probably a mere interlude. They were wiped out in a war on two fronts against the Sassanians and the Turks pushing in from the East.

The Turks are supposed to have originally come from the South Siberian frontier mountains between the Altai chain and the upper Yenisei river. The first documentary evidence referring to them dates back to the middle of the 6th century A.D. Chinese annals record that the Shuon-Shuon ruler denied his daughter's hand to T'u-Kue, head of a tribe, to whom he had promised it as a reward for his help, that T'u-Kue rose in rebellion against his faithless master with the help of another tribe, deprived him of his power, and thus himself became ruler over the eastern part of Central Asia (B. Spuler).

Nothing in this process indicates that something more far-reaching is happening than one of the numerous changes of dynasties. The Sassanians establish contact with the new masters of East Central Asia and with their help defeat the Hephtalites: they drive out the devil by Beelzebub, as Spuler puts it. With them Iran acquired neighbours who caused constant trouble for more than a thousand years, who furnished dynasties again and again, but who were assimilated culturally and not infrequently also linguistically in the process. Only now does the West of Central Asia become Turkestan, the country of the Turks. But this judgment can be all too easily misleading. In so far as the Turks became the superimposed ruling class in oases and cities, the Turkish language became generally accepted, but culturally Iran seems to have remained stronger. This is certainly due to Iran's superiority through long periods of history, and to the strong East Iranian substrate in the urban and agricultural population,* and finally to a kind of cultural shock caused by contact with the superior standard of civilization of the urban population. – The author is – with K. Otto-Dorn (Kalter 1982, Otto-Dorn 1979) – of the opinion that the Turkic element has always been underestimated in descriptions of the development of Islamic civilization and art, and has expressed the opinion that the creation of the independent style of Islamic metalwork must have taken place mainly under Turkic influence; however, the opinion that this development is due to a symbiosis of Turkic and East Iranian elements cannot be brushed aside. One thing is certain: the quality of the metalwork cannot have been achieved by migrating artisans – it cannot have been created in the steppes. It seems equally certain to this author that the taste and the demand of the ruling class, i. e. also of the patrons of art, had a strong influence on the products of the artisans. (The same phenomenon recurs in recent manufactures). Something that helps to support these hypotheses may be seen in the strikingly numerous representations of animals; these cannot find their explanation in Iranian pictorial traditions (Kalter 1982).

The Islamic conquest of Turkestan in the 8th century was preceded by one of the most unfortunate centuries in Central Asia's turbulent history. After having destroyed the Hephtalite Empire together with the Sassanians, the Turks tried to establish contact with Byzantium. 'In 568 Emperor Justin II received Turkish envoys who proposed that he should take over the transportation of silk, Byzantium being bypassed.' (B. Spuler). As the negotiations with Byzantium dragged on for a long time, the Turkish Khans

---

*) Research into the east Iranian Soghdian civilisation is still in its infancy. Soghdians 'never formed a large state, but settled in a plurality of small states, feudal estates, city states and villages. They were masters of metal and textile crafts. Their artists created fine temples and fortresses and Soghdian traders went to China, Byzantium, India and Iran'. B. Brentjes, 1977.

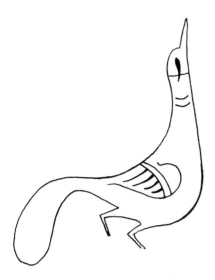
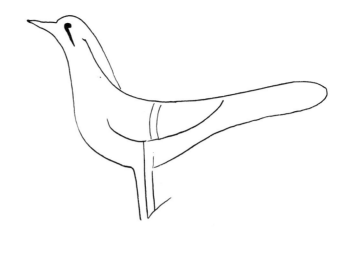

Ill. 18   Representations of birds, left from a 12th-c. Ghaznevid metal work, right from a Turkestan samovar from about 1900

were encouraged to continuous armed conflicts with the Sassanians which, however, so weakened them that they finally had to surrender to the rulers of the newly founded Chinese T'ang dynasty who pursued an expansive policy. But the Chinese had overestimated their force with this expansion to the far west. On the eve of the Islamic conquest Turkestan was split up into a great many small and minute khanates. Iran was worn down by constant fighting with Byzantium in the west and the Turks in the east. The last important impact upon the country, after mounted nomadism and the cultural traditions of the Turks, was Islam which is as much a rule of life and law as a religion. Thus it was politically superior to the religions previously existing there, such as shamanism and the Manichaeism of the Turks, and the religions of Zoroaster, Buddhism, and Nestorian Christianity which were mainly to be found in the West. The further cultural and historical development is set within the framework provided by mounted nomadism, Turkic traditions, and Islam.

At the time of Muhammad's death, in 632 A.D., his followers, the Muslims, ruled over the Arab peninsula. His successors, the first four 'Rightful Caliphs', expanded the Muslim Arabs' sphere of influence to Syria, Egypt, and Iran. Iran had collapsed relatively quickly. The Islamic conquest of Iran began in 636; in 651 the last of the Sassanian Shahs was killed in his last fortress at Merv. His son Peroz called on the Chinese for help, who confirmed him as governor of Po-sse (Persia). The Arabs' further advance had come to a standstill because of civil wars in the central regions; these preceded the foundation of the Umayyad Caliphate. So the Arabs contented themselves with separate raids from their base at Merv.

In 659 the Chinese had brought Transoxania and the region between the Oxus and Indus rivers under their control, when they were unexpectedly attacked by strong units of Tibetan nomads who occupied the Tarim basin, cutting off the new western provinces from the centre of China. These had to be given up in 674. The Arabs tried to profit from this political vacuum by settling 50,000 Arab families at Merv and by thrusts into Bukhara. The Arab conquest turned out to be difficult because the country was scattered with numerous small independent fortresses; there was no central fort that could have been conquered. The inhabitants of the steppes avoided contact with the Arabs by withdrawing into the immensity of that vast region. In 694, the Chinese were able to win back the Tarim basin from the Tibetans. From 697 on, a grandson of the last Sassanian Shah tried as Chinese governor of Tohkaristan (parts of eastern West Turkestan) to restore his ancestors' empire.

The second successful Arab wave of invasion started in 705. First Bukhara was conquered, then in 710–712 the Amu Darya valley, and in 713 the Arab conquerors appeared in the Ferghana valley. The assassination of the Arab general (715) as a consequence of dynastic quarrels at the court of the Caliph enabled the Chinese for the last time to stabilize their power in Turkestan. The violence of a Chinese general induced the inhabitants of Samarkand to turn for help to Abu Muslim, the Muslim ruler of East Iran. It was in the battle of Talas, in 751, that the Muslims won the decisive victory that permanently secured Turkestan for Islam. – An important side effect for cultural history is the fact that amongst the prisoners taken during the course of that battle were artisans who knew how to make paper. From these the Muslims took over the art of making paper, first at Samarkand – no doubt an essential contribution to the rise of learning and art in the Islamic world. It was also Muslims who made papermaking known in Europe.

During the next 150 years, Turkestan was subject to Arab administration, which was characterized by constant troubles and revolts of the population fighting for their independence. The descendants of the Arab conquerors were almost completely assimilated.

Only in the 9th century did independent Islamic states emerge in Turkestan, at first still formally dependent on the court of the Caliph. The most important of these states, culturally as well as economically, was the Samanid Empire (874–999). The dynasty takes its name from a landlord, Saman who came from Balkh in North Afghanistan. The Samanids' capital was Bukhara, their most important governor's seat was Nishapur. With the help of Turkish military slaves, the Samanids built up a strictly organized army. The organization of a most efficient civil administration which was conducted by ten ministries (divans) resulted in a prospering trade and agriculture. Long-distance trade was possible on the routes that had become safe again. As is documented by tens of thousands of Samanid coins found in Scandinavia, but also a few scattered ones in Central Europe, Samanid trade, passing via the Volga basin, reached nearly the whole of Europe. The list of export goods made up by the Arab geographer Mukadasi in the 10th century (Brentjes 1976) is long and impressive. His (incomplete) list comprises: rugs and prayer rugs from Bukhara and Samarkand, fine cloths and weavings made of wool, cotton and silk, soap, make-up, consecration oil, bows that could only be bent by the strongest men, swords, armour, stirrups, fittings, saddles, quivers, tents, raisins, sesame, nuts, honey, sheep, cattle, horses and hawks, iron, silver, sulphur, copper.

The wealth which was mainly caused by foreign trade led to a rise in the demand for artisans' high quality products. Artisans of the Samanid period made an essential contribution to the development of Islamic ceramics. At the Samanid court flourished learned men known throughout the world like the philosopher and physician Ibn Sina (the Avicenna of the Occident), the mathematician and scientist al Biruni, and distinguished poets and founders of Iranian literary traditions like Rudaki and above all Firdausi who, however, was to finish his Shahnameh only at the court of the Turkish Ghaznevids and is often called 'the Homer of the Iranians'. During the rule of the Samanid Emirs, who were continually fighting against the infidel Turks, orthodox Sunnite Islam was accepted in their sphere of influence. On the whole, the Samanid period was of outstanding importance for the creation and development of East Islamic culture. The reason for the destruction of the flourishing state of the Samanids was again its inner instability which was a consequence of the fact that the dynastic succession was, as in all Islamic states, unscheduled. Thanks to his capability, a Turkish slave officer named Alptigin rose to the rank of commander in chief of the army in Khorassan. In the course of succession quarrels he rebelled against his Samanid masters (962 A.D.) and took the town of Ghazni which was to become the centre of the first Turkic-Islamic great empire in history. At the peak of its power, around the middle of the 11th century, this empire covered an area that stretched from North East Iran over Turkestan, the Afghanistan of today to Pakistan and North India. In the meantime the Samanid Empire had been attacked by Turkic (probably Karluk) peoples from the east, so that everything was in a state of disorder. They had been converted to Islam since the middle of the century which is why they were not offered any serious resistance by the population of the Samanid Empire. In 999, the Samanid Empire collapsed and was divided up among the Karakhanids, i. e. the masters of the Karluks, and the Ghaznevids. The main focus inside the Eastern Caliphate had shifted from Turkestan to the heart of the Ghaznevid Empire in North Afghanistan. Turkic cultural elements, combined already during the Samanid Empire with others from ancient Iran and enriched by Indian forms and ideas, are at the origin of a development which will come to full bloom only under the successors of the Ghaznevids – the Seljuks, also a Turkic group.

The Ghaznevids themselves had initiated that development. The Seljuks, 'a branch of the Turkic tribe of the Oghuz' (Hambly), had left their grazing grounds near the mouth of the Syr Darya and had advanced towards the south, led by their ruler who had converted to Islam. Sultan Mahmud of Ghazni arrested the son of Seljuk – the latter had died in the meantime – and banished him to India, but he allowed the tribe to cross the Oxus. The leaders of that migration became emirs at Merv and Nishapur and inflicted a crushing defeat upon Mahmud's successor Masud in the battle of Dandankan (1041). The Ghaznevids lost Khorassan to the Seljuks, and the centre of their empire shifted to North India; Ghazni, however, was to remain its capital for another 110 years. There was nothing to prevent the Turks from conquering Iran nor was there a reason why the seat of the Caliphate should not be shifted to Baghdad. The Sultans of the Great Seljuks, regarding themselves as defenders of orthodox Islam, penetrated into Asia Minor in their fight with Byzantium and established the Sultanate of Rum (1071, Rum Seljuks), which was the root of the most important Islamic-Turkic empire of history – the Ottoman Empire. The Turkmen people is said to have been part of the tribal unit of the Oghuz, according to 11th-century sources (Mahmud of Kashgar).

Seljuk rule brought nearly two centuries of quiet to the central regions of Iran. In Turkestan, the Seljuk sphere of influence was divided between the Ghorids, formerly vassals of Ghazni, who had succeeded to the Ghaznevids in Afghanistan after 1151, and the Kara-Khitai, a pagan Mongol group. The Ghorids' and Kara-Khitai's enemies were the Seljuk governors of Turkestan, the Khorezmshahs, who won predominance over the whole of Khorassan in 1210. From their capital Samarkand, they ruled an empire that stretched from the Pamir in the east to the western part of Iraq, and were for two decades the predominant power of the eastern Islamic world. The assassination of 450 Muslim merchants who were on their way back from a trade journey to Mongolia, by the governor of the Khorezmshahs at Otrar in 1218, and the execution of an envoy of Chingiz-Khan were the last reasons for the Mongol invasion, one of the most cruel nomad campaigns that ever swept across Turkestan.

Originally, the name Mongol was used to designate only a small tribe which lived south-east of Lake Baikal and which was ethnically and linguistically related to Turkic and Tungus peoples. The leaders of the Mongols and their neighbouring tribes were khans who formed a kind of steppe aristocracy. Temuchin, who was to become Chingiz-Khan (1155–1227), the founder of the Mongol Empire, the impoverished son of a khan, is said to have been a charismatic leader figure. After many years of fighting he finally managed to unite the tribes of his native country under his leadership. In 1206 he was elected Great Khan of that confederation at a grand assembly, the kuriltay. He adopted the title Kha-Khan (highest khan) and the name Chingiz-Khan, and the whole confederation adopted the name Mongols. Chingiz-Khan set up a strict body of laws called yassa and created a rigidly organized nomad army, which was divided into units of 10,000, 1,000, 100 and 10 men, each with a leader at the top who, in the case of the greater units, was personally chosen by Chingiz-Khan.* In 1207 he already commanded an army of 120,000 horsemen. One of Chingiz-Khan's main concerns was unhindered trade through the steppes. This is why the assassination of the merchants at Otrar resulted in a campaign with a troop strength of 150,000 to 200,000 men which led to the defeat first of Otrar, in 1220 of Bukhara, shortly after of Samarkand. Chingiz-Khan went to winter quarters with the main body of his army at the bank of the Amu Darya. In spring 1221 he took Balkh, his youngest son Tolui sacked Herat, Merv and Nishapur.

The judgments of Chingiz-Khan's personality and deeds differ greatly. 'The heritage left by "Satan's scorching sun" and "the Scourge of God", as Chingiz-Khan had called himself at Bukhara, was an empire that stretched from the coasts of China to the Caspian Sea, but in which all civilization and nearly all life were exterminated. Even the oasis regions of Transoxania along the banks of the Amu and Syr Darya, renowned for their fertility, were com-

pletely devastated, Bukhara, Samarkand, Tashkent – cities that were known far beyond the boundaries of Central Asia for their prospering trade and especially for their culture – were laid in ruins, and the former "Great Silk Route" was no longer a pulsating trade route in that wilderness, but only a supply base for the Mongols rushing to the west.' (Pander 1982). Hambly, on the other hand, quotes a contemporary Arab historian: 'Neither historians nor biographers have ever reported a dynasty that was blessed with so much obedience on the part of its subjects and soldiers as this victorious Mongol dynasty. Verily, the civil as well as the military obedience with which it was blessed is such as was never enjoyed by any other dynasty.' 'The *pax mongolica* was a reality which made it possible to travel in relative security from the Crimea as far as Korea, and which enabled not only trade goods, but also ideas and inventions to get from one end of the then known world to the other.'

No matter how the Mongol rule may be judged, one thing which is certain is the fact that Islamic art received – particularly under the successors of Chingiz-Khan – a wealth of stimulating influences, mainly from China, the after-effects of which could be felt long after the Mongol period.

The casualties caused by the Mongol campaigns were terribly high. For Turkestan and Iran alone, the death toll is estimated to about five million. For the sake of historical justice it must however be said that a huge mounted army is extremely vulnerable, and that killing the population was almost a necessity in order to survive oneself. Hambly assesses Chingiz-Khan's personality as follows: 'His cruelty may in its way not have been worse that that of his contemporaries, the Dzhürtshit, the Khorezmshahs, or the leaders of the Albigensian Wars in Europe. In that respect he was entirely a man of his time, but he never stained his name with senseless sadism.' Hambly has also pointed to 'the greater institutional stability and viability' of all post-Mongolian Muslim dynasties (the Moghuls, Safavids, Ottomans) and supposes that this is due to a survival of Mongol traditions. On the other hand it is certain that the proportion of the sedentary population to the nomads shifted lastingly in favour of the latter.

Chingiz-Khan died after a fall from his horse in 1227, during a campaign in North China. His empire was divided amongst his sons. The Tarim basin and Transoxania were Tshagatay's ulus (i. e. part of the empire). Under his and his successors' rule Central Asia went through a period of relative quiet. In that part of the Empire Islam was made the state religion in 1333. In the regions south and west of the Amu Darya and in present-day Iran the Empire of the Il-Khans emerged under Mongol princes. For three quarters of a century, this was one of the most powerful empires of the Middle East, especially after Baghdad, the seat of the Caliphate, had succumbed to the Mongol attack in 1258.

*) Even today the names used for the ranks of officers in the Turkish army are onbashi, yüsbashi and bimbashi (leader of a group of ten, a hundred or a thousand).

Ill. 19   Courtyard of the caravanserai at Merv, before 1890

Magnificent buildings and small objects of the highest quality give evidence of the quick rise of Iran under the rule of the Il-Khans.

Once again a great nomad empire rose from the soil of Central Asia. Its founder, Timur Lenk (Timur the Lame, or Tamerlane, as he used to be called in Europe), born in 1336 as a son of a Turkish emir near Shahrisabs, spent his youth, like his great example, Chingiz-Khan, as leader of a band of adventurers and robbers. During the years 1363–70 he tried, with varying fortunes of war, to take the province of Mawarannahr (the ancient Greek province of Transoxania). In 1370 he managed to steal the region round Balkh from his brother-in-law, Husain. He chose Samarkand as his residence and made it a metropolis. An idea of the devasting force of his campaigns may best be gained from the following synoptic table (after Hambly).

c. 1370–80	Period of consolidation in Mawarannahr. Campaigns in Moghulistan and Khorezm
1380–82	Incursion into Khorassan. Capture of Herat
1383	Capaigns in Khorassan and Seistan
1384–85	Campaigns in western Khorassan, Massanderan, and West Iran. Capture of Ray and Sultanijeh
1386–88	Campaigns in Luristan, Azerbaijan, Georgia, East Anatolia, and Fars. Sack of Isfahan, capture of Shiras (1387)
1388–91	Campaigns against the Golden Horde. Sack of Urgench (1388)
1392–94	Campaigns in Fars, Mesopotamia, Anatolia, Georgia. Capture of Baghdad (1393)
1395	Second campaign against the Golden Horde
1398–1401	Incursion into North India. Sack of Delhi (1398). Campaigns against Georgia, against the Dzhalayrids and the Mamelukes of Egypt. Capture of Sivas and Aleppo (1400). Sack of Damascus and Baghdad (1401)

Ill. 20   Lotus blossoms, left from a Timurid metal work, right from a 19th-c. Turkestan pot

1402	The Ottoman Sultan Bajezid I defeated and taken prisoner in Ankara. Sack of Bursa and Izmir
1404–05	Incursion intended into China. Death of Timur (1405)

At Timur's death his empire extended from the Indus to the Mediterranean. His son Shahruck emerged victorious from violent wars of succession. Reigning from Herat over Khorassan and the Afghanistan of today, he was one of the greatest patrons of the arts ever to have sat on an Islamic throne. His son Ulugh-beg resided as governor at Samarkand. He was himself an eminent man of learning – historian, mathematician, and astronomer – and drew a great number of learned men to his court. Both of them were enthusiastic supporters of Sunnite Islam and founded important madrassas (theological colleges). Politically, the rule of the Timurids was not much more than a short, if imposing interlude for Turkestan. Culturally – with regard to the development of architecture, poetry, the arts of the book and painting, and also for the so-called decorative arts – the importance of the Timurid period cannot be overestimated. Forms and ornaments which appeared in their characteristic shape for the first time in the Timurid period have dominated the traditions of the arts and crafts until well into our century. Constant rivalries for the succession to the throne attended the decay of Timurid power and the rise of the last of the Turkic great powers in Turkestan, the Uzbeks.

The first important Uzbek ruler of Turkestan, Muhammad Sheyban, was born around the year 1451. Son of a khan, he spent his youth after his father's death as a freebooter and united a number of khanates into which Timur's heritage had disintegrated. Here the historical dynamic which was effective in the emergence of the Mongol Empire repeats itself – for the last time and on a smaller scale – with the Uzbeks. Around 1500 Sheyban was in possession of Bukhara and Samarkand, where he drove out Babur, the founder of the Moghul dynasty. By 1505 he had conquered Tashkent, the Ferghana valley, Balkh and Kunduz. After the death of the Timurid ruler Husayn Baykara he managed to take the Timurids' last stronghold, Herat, without meeting resistance. He had to give up his intended march to India because of pressure from Kazakh troups at the northern frontier of his empire. A much more dangerous enemy, however, had arisen with the new dynasty of the Safavids (1501/2–1722).

After the fall of the Il-Khans Iran had distintegrated into several small territories. From the middle of the 13th century on, there had been fights in North Iran between two Turkmen clans who were at enmity with each other, the Kara Qoyonlu (Black Sheep) and the Ak Qoyonlu (White Sheep); the latter finally emerged victorious. Incidentally, the rule of these Turkmen units in North Iran and Mesopotamia was the only case of foundations of states of any importance undertaken by Turkmen. Sheikh Safi ad Din from Ardebil (1252–1334), from whom the Safavid dynasty takes its name, had – under Ak Qoyonlu who at that time was still a Sunnite – founded a Dervish order which was given a strict military organization and dressed in uniform under his successors, from the middle of the 15th century on. The most conspicuous element of the

Ill. 21   Lotus blossom runner from a samovar, c. 1900

units, which in the meantime had become Shiite, was their red cap. It was the Kyzylbash (Redheads), led by the first Safavid Shah, Ismail, who defeated the Ak Qoyonlu and took Tabriz in 1501. The Safavids, who had come to power with Turkmen aid, were the first Iranian dynasty after the Islamic conquest to rule over the whole territory of the Iran of today. They founded the Iranian national state committed to Shiite Islam. The fights against their strictly Sunnite neighbours, the Uzbeks, and against the Ottomans who were also Sunnites were, it is true, fights for land and power, but they were at the same time fierce religious wars. Muhammad Sheyban was killed in 1510 in a battle against the Safavids. The separation of Turkestan from the rest of the Sunnite Islamic world by the Safavids was certainly one of the decisive reasons for the decline into insignificance of a region that had been one of the historically most important parts of the Islamic world.

Muhammad Sheyban's death set off the wars of succession customary in the Islamic sphere in such cases. Only in 1583 did Abdullah, probably the greatest of the Sheybanid Khans, succeed in uniting the whole of Turkestan, with the exception of Khiva. He made Bukhara his residence, tried to intensify trade, handicraft and agriculture by building caravanserais, canals, bridges and madrassas, and to continue the old cultural traditions. The architecture of the time, like art in general, follows Timurid traditions. Timurid standard, however, was rarely achieved. After Abdullah's death the Sheybanid Empire disintegrated into a great many small principalities. Tashkent and Samarkand fell into the hands of the Kazakhs who were supported by Czarist Russia. The other khanates, including Khiva in the 18th century, remained under Uzebek rule until the Russian conquest, and some of them continued to do so as protectorates until power was taken over by the Soviets (1920). Besides the Tadzhiks, the Uzbeks have been the greatest population group in Turkestan since the time of the first Sheybanid Khan. It was they who finally turkicized Turkestan, at least linguistically. Culturally, they partly assimilated to the old-established Iranian (Tadzhik) population. The mixed culture which emerged from this inter-assimilation, the culture of the cities of Turkestan, cannot be ascribed to any single population group. Wherever on the following

pages urban material is designated as Uzbek, the author follows information given by the previous owners or, where this is lacking, he passes on the attribution generally made in literature. (With such material, Tadzhik provenance should always be taken into consideration).

In conclusion, let us recapitulate the stages of Turkestan's history that made the most important impact on its civilization:

Events of greatest importance were the Indo-Aryan (Iranian) immigration wave in the second half of the second millennium B.C.; the emergence of mounted nomadism after the beginning of the first millennium B.C.; the Turkicizing of Turkestan which begins in the 5th century A.D.; and the Islamization from the 7th century A.D. on.

Events of secondary importance with differing impact were the formation of the Samanid Empire, an Iranian-Turkic mixed culture; the Mongol invasion in the 13th century; the Timurid Empire in the 14th century with the formation of a lasting cultural tradition; and the penetration by the Uzbeks, i. e. the final Turkicizing of Turkestan from the 15th century on. The conquest of Turkestan by Czarist Russia and the subsequent Sovietization brought about a break with the cultural traditions of the region, in spite of the efforts of Soviet cultural policy after World War II.

One question has often been asked, and different answers have been given: what are the reasons for the decline of Turkestan as a centre of political power, also in comparison with other regions of the Islamic world in which it began later and was less dramatic? Apart from the above-mentioned isolation of Turkestan by Shiite Iran a decisive factor was certainly the discovery of the sea route to India. This led to a decrease of the transcontinental trade which at the beginning was hardly felt, but which quickly grew worse; in the 19th century trade was practically brought to a standstill, which deprived the Turkestan towns of a considerable part of their economic basis. The decline of long-distance trade was accelerated by the splitting up of Turkestan after the breakdown of the Uzbek Sheybanid Empire near the end of the 16th century. The consequences were insecurity of the trade routes because the small states were no longer able to protect the caravans effectively against raids of predatory nomads, and the increase of trade impediments through customs duties that were often fixed at random in each of the small states. The decline may further have been accelerated by the intellectual climate which was dominated by the mullahs who had become fanatic and bigoted as a consequence of their diaspora situation. It has also been pointed out that the rulers of Turkestan had too much confidence in the superiority of quick mounted armies and neglected the development of modern warfare. All their neighbours had introduced firearms and artillery before the Turkestan Khans and Emirs followed their example. Armies which approached territor-

Ill. 22   Sart cotton spinners, before 1890

Ill. 23   Teke amulet in the shape of a double-headed eagle after the model of the Tsarist double-headed eagle

ies on foot during the Russian conquest are reported to have been reproachably underestimated by those territories' rulers. The conquest of Turkestan caused a few hundred casualities on the Russian side, but thousands on the side of the Turkestan defenders.

Due to the political decay of Turkestan and its shift from the centre of a huge world empire in the 14th century to an isolated peripheral situation, late medieval cultural traditions survived until our own time. This makes the study of the recent cultures of Turkestan so fertile, but at the same time so difficult; they can only be understood from a historical point of view.

Ill. 24   Yurt door, with chip carving décor from the environs of Aqcha.
145 cm by 82 cm

Settlements and Dwellings

The geographer, E. Grötzbach (1972) has given us a highly detailed picture of the manifold changes that have taken place in the settlements of north-east Afghanistan since the nineteenth century. It may be assumed that the structure of Turkestan settlements has changed considerably in what is today Soviet territory since the Russian colonization, and in Afghanistan with increasing rapidity since the thirties of the present century.

Most of our knowledge of old Turkestan towns comes from accounts handed down to us by numerous nineteenth-century travellers (e. g. H. Vambéry, F. v. Schwarz, H. Moser-Charlottenfels) who described them in great detail. The structure of the great old cities of 'Russian-Turkestan' has been preserved because the Russian colonists founded their new towns near the walls of the old cities. However, we know a great deal less about the old structure of rural settlements because they hardly attracted early travellers. Descriptions of nomadic settlements are also rare but correspond to observations still made today.

We have detailed descriptions of urban and rural dwellings and yurts, the round felt tents used by the nomads. They indicate that little has changed in this respect. The religiously based sanctity and inviolability of the domestic sphere which were stressed by each of the early travellers, have, like female dress, proved to be the most stable element of Turkestan's material culture – a feature, incidentally, found in most regions of the Islamic Orient.

Turkmen Camps

Turkmen tent settlements are known as 'auls'. The tent, 'öy' in Turkmen, is known as: 'yurt' (which originally meant the place on which the tent was built) or 'kibitka'. The aul consists of the yurts of related, economically interdependent groups (clans). In groups which are still nomadic, the yurts stand in straight rows with the door-openings facing south, or in a shallow curve opening southwards (according to Karutz). In northern Afghanistan orientation has been observed (M. Centlivres)* to change with the season (to the east in winter). The assertion of some authors that the door opening faces towards Mecca has not been substantiated.

Yurts are circular, collapsible and transportable huts (see Ill. 25) with a dome-like (e. g. for the Turkmen) or conical roof. Besides the so-called 'black tent', the yurt is the most widespread form of dwelling used by nomads. It is found in a 7,000-km long region stretching from central Anatolia right up to Mongolia and southern Siberia, and is used by all nomadic Turkish and Mongol peoples – in Afghanistan also by groups culturally influenced by these such as the Tadzhiks, Hazarahs and Aymaqs.

The history of the yurt is known only in rough outline. Herodotus reports that the Scythians travelled through the steppes in clumsy caravans. William of Rubruck, a Franciscan friar, who, in the 13th century, was sent by the French king to the court of Bathu-Khan, reports on round huts which were lifted whole on to ox arts. The present latticework panel yurts of the type still used today were first described by Carpini – also in the 13th century.

'A yurt consists of the following main elements:
1. A wooden frame: latticework panels, roof struts, roof ring, door frame with or without door leaf.
2. Felt covering
3. Woven bands and ropes made of wool and cotton (Author's note: the use of cotton is certainly a recent development) which hold the wooden structure together and serve to fasten the felt covering.' (M. Centlivres)

A Turkmen yurt in possession of the Linden Museum, Stuttgart, consists of four latticework panels which, when fully pulled out, are 138 cm high. The poles of these panels are bound together with strips of animal hide (cow or camel). The yurt diameter ranges between 450 cm and 600 cm (Peter A. Andrews reports of a yurt of 12 m diameter) and may be easily varied by pulling out the panel to its full size or by contracting it. The height of the yurt then varies accordingly, and this usually ranges between 300 and 400 cm in the centre. An opening is left in the panel for the two-leaf door (with carvings mostly on the inside – see Ill. 24) set on two pins in two sockets in the lintel and the threshold.

The number of roof struts ranges from 40 to 100, depending on the size of the yurt. (In our example, there are 74 struts 260 cm long). The struts are bent at the lower end and rest on the tips of the panel where they are secured with woollen strips. The upper ends are inserted into the holes of the roof ring. The diameter of the ring is 80–180 cm as a rule, though ours is 215 cm. The frame is covered with seven pieces of felt. The airing hole in the dome is also covered with a piece of felt during the night or when it rains, and it can be opened and closed from outside

*) M. Centlivres gives the most detailed recent description of the manufacture, equipping and distribution of yurts. The historical data are based on F. Kussmaul.

Ill. 25 Camels with dismantled yurts at Aul Kurtli near Ashkhabad, 1929

by means of a woollen rope. The pieces of felt are fastened with woollen ropes which are sewn onto them. Outside, the latticework panel is covered with reed mats. Panel and roof struts are held together by woven woollen bands decorated with bright patterns. These are part of the ornamentation of the yurt and are one of the many imaginative and varied woven (kelim or gilim) decorative elements made by the Turkmen. On festive occasions, wealthy families use extremely wide bands (see Ill. 34: 54 cm wide) with knotted ornamentation. These are not required for structural purposes and have decorative and possibly magical functions. These bands are luxuries and clearly indicate the wealth of the tent owner. Andrews maintains that they take from one to three years to make.

A yurt may have no door. A felt curtain or carpet may be used instead.

The yurt frame – mostly of osier, more rarely of popular

– is made by a non-nomadic carpenter from whom it is acquired by purchase or barter. The felts, like the tent webbing, are made by the women of the family. W. König describes how they are made: 'The carefully beaten and cleaned wool was spread out in several layers on a reed mat (gamysh), dampened and rolled up in the mat. The roll thus produced was tied tightly and rolled on the earth for an extended period and frequently drenched with cold water. Once the felt mass attained the required density, it was taken out of the mat and rolled out flat again for one to two hours. This exhausting work was performed by three or four women who, on their knees, rolled out the damp felt with their lower arms, back and forth on the mat which served as a pad.' Today, yurts are still made for bridal couples by Afghan Turkmen groups which are in fact no longer nomadic. M. Centlivres reports that the bridegroom's father provides the wooden frame and the felt covering while the bride's father has the women in his family make the bands and supplies the household effects.

Yurts can be optimally adapted to climatic conditions,

Ill. 26   Teke Turkmen with decorated horse outside a yurt, before 1890

so even non-nomadic Turkmen prefer them in summer to the hot, suffocating clay huts. In northern Afghanistan one can see them everywhere within the walls of the court enclosures, standing next to the clay houses. In summer, guests are welcomed in yurts. The felt is 0.5–1.5 cm thick so it keeps out the wind; the grease in the wool keeps out water. In summer the felt is partly folded back, and curtains which are rolled up in the daytime are used instead of doors.

Despite its considerable weight (the felts alone weigh up to 130 kg, the total weight of a yurt is about 250–300 kg), a yurt can be built up and dismantled with surprising rapidity. Three or four women can do it in half an hour. Even the earliest travellers report with amazement how, after seeing a Turkmen aul from afar on their travels, the whole settlement had disappeared without a trace when they had reached the spot one hour later. All

the parts of a dismantled yurt can be transported on two camels. Another camel, or horses are needed to transport the household effects. Larger pieces of furniture, such as chests, are placed in position before the yurt is erected because as a rule they cannot pass through the 80-cm-wide door (Ill. 27).

Ill. 27 Chest, probably walnut with chip carved décor, made at Aqcha. Two chests form part of the furnishing of the yurt or livingroom of the house of north Afghan Turkmen. H. 119 cm, l. 163 cm, w. 65 cm

The Interior of the Yurt

The interior of the yurt is subdivided in accordance with very strict rules by all the peoples using them, though these rules may vary from group to group. In the centre of the tent or somewhat shifted towards the door, there is the fireplace. In the simplest case, this is a clay basin, though stones or iron tripods may be used as well. The clay oven for bread is placed outside the yurt in summer and inside it in winter. As well as the main fireplace, there may be a small fireplace for tea water if no samovar (Ill. 33) is used. The master of the tent has his place on the right-hand side of the entrance, his bed directly behind it. The wife's area is on the left of the entrance, with her bed immediately adjacent to it. The place of honour for guests is in the middle of the rear wall directly facing the entrance.

The interior of a yurt is an extremely colourful, cheerful sight. A comparison of my collection of notes and interrogation results obtained during my trip to north Afghanistan in 1978 with the reports of various other travellers and colleagues indicates that the basic subdivision of the interior is everywhere the same as described above, but that there are considerable regional or, perhaps, tribal differences in furnishing details. The following description is based on the autor's notes*) to make it more stimulating reading.

Two narrow tent bands hang down crossed from the yurt sky beneath the ceiling. According to the information given by older persons, a hundred years ago (i. e. a very long time ago?) these were pure silk embroideries (similar to those shown in Ill. 96). Wealthy families had Russian printed fabrics spanned beneath the entire dome. The rear

---

*) The furnishing described is of an ideal type. It is the result of observation and questioning. The informants were obviously trying to be as detailed as possible in their answers. As the Turkmen gradually became settled, knotted or kelim bags were replaced by tin chests or shelves that could be bought in any bazaar.

46

wall may be decorated with a couple of loosely worked 'ku-rachis' (patchwork curtains) which are also used to decorate the flanks of the bridal camel for the wedding procession (Ill. 124). Kurachis of this type are also found amongst the Uzbeks. According to the information given to me, the ma-terials are purchased at town bazaars and made up by the women of the family. The patchwork may also be embroi-dered or decorated with down feathers, horsehair, buttons or blue glass beads sewn on. (The blue beads may be amu-lets against the evil eye.)

At the latticework panels on the right and left-hand si-des of the entrance, there hang 'chovals', extremely large storage bags made of knotted or kelim fabrics. There are also kelim chovals with knotted strips (on the average 60–95 cm high by 100–170 wide). These, I was told, are mostly used for storing clothes. Depending on the size of the yurt and the bags, there may be 6–10 bags hanging insi-de. These bags are also called 'torba' or 'mafrash' depend-ing on their shape and function. Mafrashes are 25–30 cm high and 70–90 cm wide, and according to Azadi, they must have been used exclusively for storing women's uten-sils. The width of a torba is on the average the same as that of a choval, the height varies from about 20 to 60 cm. As a rule, two torba bags must be made of kelim weave, the others may be knotted. Each bag is for a particular type of provisions or utensil (e. g. ammunition, meat, corn, spoons, salt, small tools for making carpets, etc.*). Often, fewer bags are needed than could actually be hung on the lattice-work. In this case, knotted strips in torba form without a rear piece are hung as decorations. Tools such as whisks, sheepshears in the sheath (Ill. 10) and so on, may also be hung directly on the latticework panel. On the rear wall fa-cing the door there hang a pair of bags known as 'ok bash' which are used to decorate the ends of the bundled roof struts when travelling. The entrance is sometimes decorated with a knotted frame (kapunuk), a practice which according to Azadi is particularly widespread amongst the Ersari.

The yurt floor is covered with one-colour or patterned felts. Knotted carpets or kelims are spread on top of these to welcome guests. As a rule, the furnishing is said to in-clude two small rugs as well as one main carpet about eight square meters in size.

On the right and left-hand sides of the door there stand two chests decorated with chip carving, which are opened by removing a board from the front. One chest contains je-wellery and valuables, the other the 'good' dishes. The bed-ding is kept on top of the chests during the daytime. This consists of the 'toshak', a sort of mattress filled with cotton

Ill. 28 Large baking bowl and spoon; sheet of metal for baking bread, all from Tashqurgan, northern Afghanistan. D. baking bowl: 55 cm, l. spoon: 36 cm; d. metal sheet: 46 cm

and covered with ikat or printed cloth, and similarly made quilts and pillows. In the women's section of the yurt, next to and under the chest, there are wooden baking dishes, bowls and vessels made of ceramics, copper or cast iron, and cooking pots. On the men's side are kept saddles, bri-dles and weapons. Large, sideboard-like pieces of painted furniture are found only amongst the Yomut.

In wealthier households, light was provided by oil-lamps made of ceramics or cast iron, with a cotton wick (today, petroleum lamps are used everywhere instead of these). Storage containers for oil were made of goat-skin or of a mixture of grass and lime. Ceramic jugs were more ra-rely used (Ill. 29).

Nomads usually had waterbags made of leather. Amongst the sedentary and semi-sendentary Turkmen of northern Afghanistan I saw bell-shaped water containers made of ceramics, about 120 cm deep, with a maximum diameter of 80 cm, which were sunk into the ground. Water jugs may be made of ceramics, but copper and brass are also used. People wash themselves after dark in front of the yurt. Ill. 30 shows a typical jug for washing. The bowl and jug washing set (Ill. 52), of the type found in urban hou-seholds, is to be found only in the homes of high-ranking and wealthy Turkmen.

The work of looking after the animals and the process-ing of animal products is performed almost exclusively by

---

*) The bags help to keep the yurt tidy and are also used when travelling. A more important consideration is undoubtedly that valuable items of the household effects stay hidden from the gaze of visitors – an intelligible point in a one-roomed dwelling.

women, so that everything connected with these is found in the women's section of the yurt. Besides ropes and pegs for tying animals, there are flat-shaped baskets (Ill. 48) for collecting the dung which is used as fuel, and also milk cans and churns made of leather, gourds or ceramics (Ill. 7). Amongst the sedentary and semi-sedentary groups of northern Afghanistan – from whom originate most of the household effects published in this book – ceramics have now virtually replaced the leather vessels which were more typical for nomads.

Wool finishing and processing is also women's work. We have already described how felt is made. Turkmen women spend every moment they can spare from looking after the animals, and their maternal and family duties, in processing wool. The wool must be cleaned with a comb and spun. Comb and spindle therefore belong to the women's side of the yurt. Wool processing, the weaving of kelims and tent bands, the knotting of carpets are performed in front of the yurt, at least in summer.

So much for my field notes on the furnishings of the yurt. If one remembers that normally not less than four people live in a yurt, it may well be imagined that it is not only full of life but also cramped. In the past, therefore, wealthy families frequently had three yurts: the normal family yurt, a yurt for guests and a smaller one for cooking. This custom seems to have died out in northern Afghanistan.

A few remarks seem to be in order to supplement my notes. In the entire literature dealing with the material culture of the nomads, the extreme functionalism and simplicity, sometimes even the poverty, of the nomad's furnishings are emphasized. This is doubtlessly true of small livestock nomads, without qualification. Such a statement must be qualified, however, when it is applied to groups belonging to the mounted nomads of central Asia. It is certainly likely that simple frames (as Karutz already mentioned) used in the yurt for holding household effects, were also used as packsaddles under way, and even as litters for small children and old women, hanging at the sides of the camel, were formerly the rule, whereas chests the exception. But the transportation capacity of a wealthy nomadic family certainly permitted travel with a luxury article like the chest. And luxury articles were certainly in demand. Packaging problems were ingeniously solved, as demonstrated by the special transportation box (Ill. 33) used for packing valuable porcelain tea services. Turned wooden bowls – mostly of mulberry wood – or ceramics made by bazaar craftsmen (such as our bowl with yellow-green and aubergine glazing) were used only in poorer households. This last bowl comes from Tashkurgan and belongs to a

Ill. 29 Water pots, copper, and handled jug, ceramic, with embossed decor. Bazaar goods from northern Afghanistan, such as formed part of the household utensils of all ethnic groups. H. from left to right: 52 cm, 37.5 cm, 40 cm

tradition which, in this region, was taken over by the potters of the Samanid period (10th century) under the influence of Chinese ceramics. Similar bowls were also used in peasant and poorer urban households. Anyone who could afford to do so used Russian lacquered wooden bowls, or porcelain with Chinese décor (Ill. 9) or painted in bright colours and flower patterns manufactured in Russia specially for the Turkestan market, instead of plain wooden ones. A proof of how highly valued porcelain was as a status symbol is given by our Ill. 42 showing how lovingly broken porcelain was mended. Until very recently, itinerant porcelain menders were to be found at every market in northern Afghanistan. Another piece of evidence proving that nomadic Turkmen had no hesitation in taking on even heavy items if they gave them status, is our brazier (Ill. 48) with a shape familiar to us from late medieval miniatures. Glass mirrors are another item that one might not expect nomads to carry with them. For transportation, they were placed in a covered wooden frame and additional protection was provided by heavily embroidered fabric bags. (These bags are often sold as Koran bags by Afghan traders, which cannot be proved and is unlikely in view of their shape, but it helps them to sell better.)

Ill. 30   Wash can from a north Afghan Turkmen household. 40 cm

Ill. 31   2 oil lamps with blue and turquoise glazing, and an oil can from rural households in northern Afghanistan. H. 13 cm, 28 cm, 39 cm

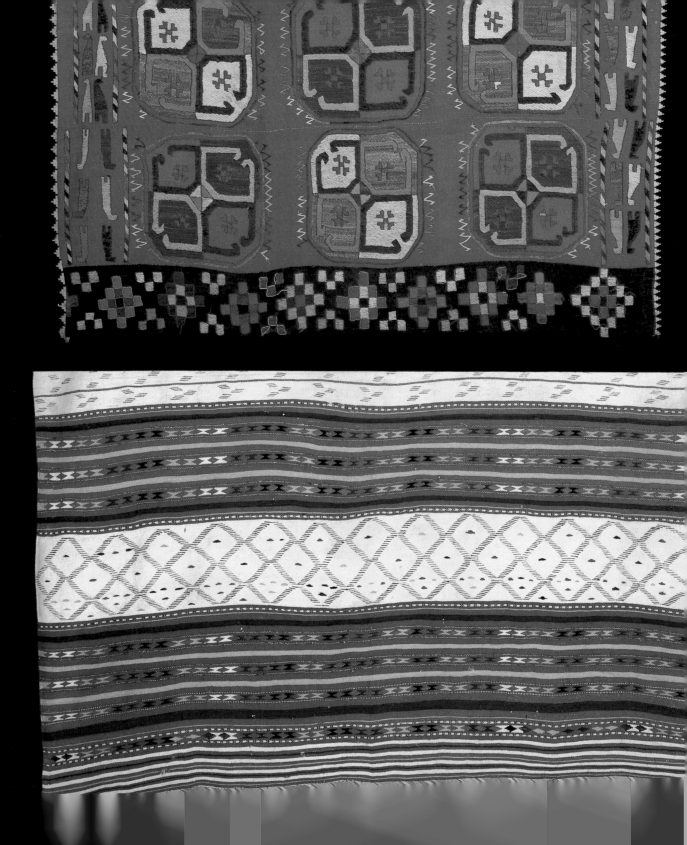

In summary it may be said that the picture presented by a Turkmen household is unusually colourful and varied. The yurt's textile furnishings, especially the various bags, which take the place of wardrobes, shelves and boxes are produced by the household itself. They were part of the bridal trousseau and the women of the bride's family often spent years working on them. Other household effects had to be acquired from traders and craftsmen by purchase or barter. So it seems likely that the possessions of a Turkmen household were frequently substantially poorer in the days before the Russian conquest of Turkestan – which introduced a monetary economy and boosted market-oriented production both in animal husbandry (Karakul sheep) and in domestic industries (carpet manufacture). This conclusion is corroborated by travellers' reports from that period.

Next two pages

Ill. 34 Decorative textile pieces from Turkestan yurts. Woven tent band with knotted décor, the most important elements of which represent trees of life, Teke Turkmen, 19th c. Below left: Lakai Uzbek embroidered tent bag and two pouches (ok bash) made in the kelim technique, and used to protect the ends of the bundled up roof struts when travelling. Otherwise, they were used to decorate the yurt, Ersari, northern Afghanistan. Below right: patchwork curtain of the type used in Turkmen and Uzbek households. When travelling, it can be used to decorate the flanks of camels. Measurements: tent band, 54 by 1,251 cm, bag, 52 by 118 cm, pouch, 70 by 32 cm, curtain, 153 by 135 cm

Ill. 32 Turkestan kelims. Top: detail of a kelim with wool embroidery; the primary ornaments are reminiscent of göls. The borders with animal decoration are noteworthy. Lakai Uzbek. Bottom: Kelim with wool embroidery from a north Afghan Turkmen group (detail). Measurements: top: 150 cm by 342 cm, bottom: 122 cm by 300 cm

Ill. 33 Transport chest, walnut (?) with chip carvings, for imported Gardener porcelain teapots, also tea bowls and a samovar, copper tinned with chased décor, Turkmen, northern Afghanistan. Chest: c. 38 by 38 by 16.5 cm, samovar: h. 52 cm

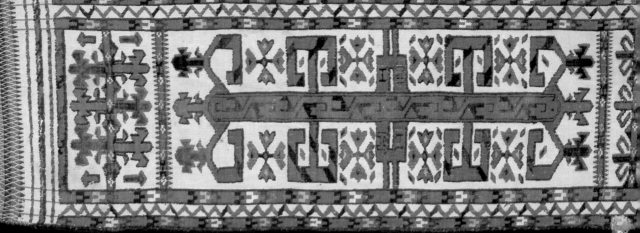

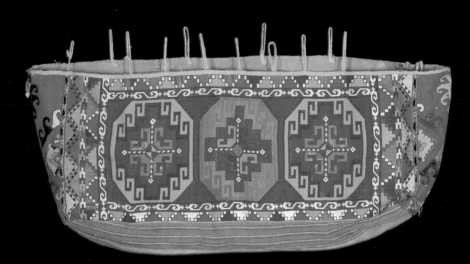

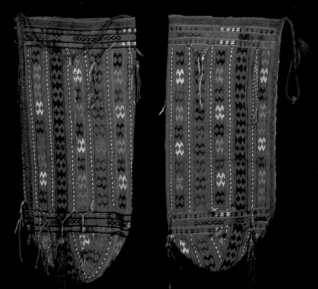

Successful participants in Alaman raids were certainly an exception to this rule. After successful adjustment to the new conditions, a certain standard of furnishing seems to have crystallized. We assume that our description applies, by and large, to the time from the turn of the century onward.

The sources relating to the distribution of craftsmen amongst the Turkmen are most unsatisfactory. From the scanty evidence given by König, the following approximate picture may be obtained:

There do not seem to have been any specialized, full-time craftsmen. König cites Vashjev 1888: '. . . a Tekin does not become a craftsman but remains a peasant who does this or that, sometimes even practising two trades simultaneously. When he works in the fields he is a farmer, and when that work is finished he is a craftsman.' Nor does König give any examples of craftsmen amongst nomadic Turkmen. He mentions non-nomadic blacksmiths, makers of agricultural implements, builders, millers, makers of smaller household utensils (copper water pots, bowls, etc.) and, surprisingly, silversmiths. The former already slight inclination towards craftwork seems to have virtually disappeared in Turkmen settlement areas after colonization and political stabilization. However that may be, the author has not succeeded in finding, for instance, coppersmith products in northern Afghanistan which can be proved to have been produced by Turkmen craftsmen. The jugs (Ill. 29 and 30), for example, were unanimously considered by all people questioned to be of local origin, but no one was prepared to assign their use to a particular ethnic group.

This means that the cultural objects of the Turkmen are obviously Turkmen in the following cases: 1. Textile products (carpets, kelims, felts, embroideries) made by Turkmen women for Turkmen households; 2. Jewellery which can be easily classified as Turkmen, even though it is often extremely difficult to assign it to particular sub-tribes. The problem of craftsmen will be discussed later. However it is most unlikely that *all* jewellery is made by Turkmen silversmiths. 3. The structural parts of the yurt and the carved doors and chests which are made by non-nomadic carvers (in Aqcha these are said to include Turkmen) as ordered by Turkmen.

Most other possessions, especially the simpler household effects originate from non-Turkmen craftsmen and are used in the same way by other peoples – Uzbeks, Tadzhiks, etc. – living in Turkestan.

We shall therefore refrain from describing simple household effects again when we turn to urban culture, and will confine ourelves to presenting the products characteristic of urban culture such as high-standard textile products and fine metalwork, plus selected examples of locally produced urban embroidery (susanis) which is as important an item of urban culture as the knotted products of the Turkmen.

Agricultural implements used by non-nomadic Turkmen are lacking in the Linden Museum collection. In other respects, the rest of the furnishings is the same as those of the yurt. So a brief description of Turkmen settlements will suffice.

In pre-colonial times, non-nomadic Turkmen lived in fortfied settlements of the clustered village type, and in 'kalas' – fortified single farmsteads surrounded by a wall with firing slits. Turkmen settlements in northern Afghanistan today tend to be linear settlements clustered around a main street, although there are also unplanned 'cluster' villages without a clear ground plan. The sites which contain the clay house, the summer yurt and a large garden (Ill. 26 gives proof that this situation existed in the last century) are surrounded by man-high clay walls. My friend and colleague, W. Böhning, who repeatedly stayed in the Turkmen region of northern Afghanistan, pointed out to me that one can walk around a Turkmen settlement for hours without seeing anything but door-covered openings in walls and every now and then a yurt dome protruding above a wall. (One can be in a Turkmen area without seeing one single Turkmen – which gives some idea of how difficult it is to work in this field.)

Ill. 35 Wooden frame of the kind hung in pairs on camels to transport household utensils while travelling, camel bell for the last animal in the caravan and large kelim transport bag (choval). Ersari Turkmen, northern Afghanistan. Frame: H. 62 cm, l. 107 cm, w. 54 cm, bell with hanger: 88 cm, bag: 70 by 110 cm

Next two pages

Ill. 36 Embroidered transport bags for mirrors and mirror in painted wood case, northern Afghanistan. The top bag comes from the Lakai Uzbek, the bottom one from the Ersari. Measurements: top bag: 33.5 by 29 cm, bottom bag: 40 by 38 cm, mirror: 33 by 25 cm

Ill. 37 Turkestan travel equipment. Transport container, left: board embroidered with cloth cover and silver ornaments. Centre: wood and leather with ornamental wire seams. The embroidered piece comes from the Lakai Uzbek, the other two were used in similar form by all Turkestan peoples. The right-hand tea bowl was imported from China, the other two are Russian Gardner porcelain, Length of containers: from 52 to 28 cm, d. of the bowls: from 10.5 to 14 cm

The clay houses with a flat roof made of poplar trunks, usually consist of one room. An additional, strongly built stable for the animals is only found in exceptional cases. As a rule this consists of nothing more than an awning made of mats and branches. Nor do all homes have kitchens: frequently only a makeshift roofed-over corner of the courtyard serves as kitchen. The house doors resemble those of the yurt in size and ornamentation. Windows are rarely glazed. When it is cold, the windows can be closed up with plain wooden shutters. The interior is divided up in the same way as described for the yurt. The furnishings used by rural Uzbek groups are so similar to that of the Turkmen that there is no need to describe them separately here.

One exception here are the fabrics made for the family's own use. As our collection impressively shows, Uzbeks and Turkmen have solved similar problems in frequently

Ill. 38   Kasa kalkan or heart-cum-rams' horns motif from an embroidered Lakai Uzbek bag.

quite different ways, despite the apparent close similarity between their traditional ornamentations and the nomadic roots shared by both cultures. It therefore seems advisable to present this material – though it gives no more than an inkling of the richly varied textile arts as practised by the rural Uzbeks – before turning to urban culture. Nothing can show more clearly than the illustrations of these specimens how far the material culture of the towns in its stock of ornamental patterns (often lightly classified as Uzbek) has developed away from the certainly even 'more primitive', original Uzbek ornamentation.

This is most obvious when one compares the textiles

from the towns with the positively archaic ornamental tradition as seen in embroidered household effects said to have been made by still nomadic or semi-nomadic groups, the Uzbek sub-tribe known as the Lakai or Laqai, and thus known as Lakai embroidery, which has come on the market in large numbers since the beginning of the seventies, probably on account of the drought which prevailed in northern Afghanistan at that time. According to Burnes and Olufsen, the Lakai lived in the eastern mountain region of the Emirate of Bukhara, and appear to have fled to northern Afghanistan to escape from the revolutionary and post-revolutionary chaos prevailing in the twenties and early thirties of this century.

Ill. 39 shows two small bags for storing small household implements, a camel head dress and an ornamental band inserted between the front edges of the bedding stacked on top of the chests. Embroideries in the same style and silver fittings can be seen in a case used for packing tea or rice bowls when travelling. Amongst the Turkmen, such cases were made of unadorned wood or leather (Ill. 37). Wonderful examples of the fine work and the brilliant colours together with severely geometric forms customary in most Lakai embroidery are the small square cloth (Ill. 165) probably used for wrapping bread, and the bag (Ill. 34) certainly used for household utensils in the tent. – The suggestion that such bags were used as cradles has not been substantiated. Like all collections, ours also poses some riddles. We mention one here, without wanting to anticipate the discussion of the highly complex problem of mutual influence exerted by the peoples of Turkestan on one another in clothing and jewellery. Ill. 85, left, shows a child's bib of the type commonly used by the Turkmen of northern Afghanistan. The embroidery in the centre is also typically Turkmen, the two lateral strips are typically Lakai. Was a Turkmen mother influenced by the colourful, but technically alien Uzbek embroidery? Or did an Uzbek woman take over a form of clothing (which to my knowledge is foreign to the Uzbeks) together with an alien ornamentation and embroidery technique? Was the item perhaps produced in one of the rare mixed marriages between Turkmen and Uzbeks? The matter is open to speculation. These questions are not posed here to make the reader feel uncertain, but to show, with one single example, how often it proves impossible to classify and label certain items with the systematic spirit required of a scientist or collector, when these come from living cultures which are constantly influencing one another.

Ill. 39   Lakai Uzbek embroideries. Top: Spoon bag and camel headdress; centre: bag-shaped wall hanging. Bottom: ornamental strips for decorating the bedding stacked on the chests. Measurements: bag, height 45 cm, Headdress, length 50 cm, wall hanging: height 25 cm, strips, width 90 cm

Ill. 40 Turned wooden bowl, ceramic bowl and wooden spoons from Tash-
kurgan, northern Afghanistan. D. wooden bowl: 31 cm, d. ceramic
bowl: 25 cm, length of spoons: 24 cm, 17 cm

A second group of Lakai embroideries is markedly different from the one presented above. The characteristic feature of the first group is a severely geometric ornamentation
covering the entire surface. In the second group, this type
alternates with a technique emphasizing outlines, with curved linear ornamentation and a decor depicting objects
(e. g. the mirror bag, Ill. 36). Both styles may appear together in one item (e. g. the bag shown in Ill. 34).

Rugs, kelims and bags, in pilework or flatweave techniques, were to be found in the homes of both nomadic Uzbeks and Turkmen, but are much more rarely represented
in western collections because they do not meet the stan-

dard of quality required in commerce. Uzbek knotted bags
in 'choval' form (Ill. 6) are much more loosely knotted than
Turkmen ones, but are quite up to their standard as far as
the clarity of the colours and variety of ornamentation are
concerned. The long, narrow kelims are characterized by
very bright colours. Their ornamentation is related to the
Turkmen göls. This similarity is also striking in kelim bags
with a décor which is often made using the highly sophisticated and difficult Sumak technique.

Ill. 41 Wooden bowl with lacquer painting and Gardener porcelain bowl.
Both were imported from Russia and were part of the inventory of
wealthy families in northern Afghanistan. D. 23.5 cm and 18.5 cm

Towns and Urban Dwellings

As pointed out in the introduction, Turkestan is a country with a great and ancient urban cultural tradition, and we described the various key functions played by the towns. Although what we said about these functions applies analogously to European as well as to Oriental towns, there are considerable differences with respect to the legal status of towns, the social structure of their inhabitants and the resulting town pattern, which will be described briefly below.*

During the Middle Ages in Europe, a class of affluent citizens without fealty to a prince emerged from the independent craftsmen and merchants organized in the town guilds. The rising bourgeoisie, in fact, strove for and acquired a great many rights (the right to mint coins, to hold markets, etc.) from the feudal lords. 'Free Imperial Towns' were autonomous, or partly autonomous, administrative units, ruled by magistrates and a mayor elected from amongst its patricians. The towns conveyed certain civil rights provided certain economic criteria were fulfilled.

As Moslems, the inhabitants of Turkestan (Islamic) towns belonged to the Umma, the community of all believers. The towns were, as we have seen, a melting pot for the most varied ethnic groups, but, besides the Islamic Sunnite majority, there were also various religious minorities. The loyalty of the inhabitants was to the extended family, or at least to the respective ethnic or religious group. Accordingly, members of such groups lived together in separate quarters, often enclosed by a surrounding wall with gates to keep them sequestered from neighbouring quarters, with their own mosque, public baths and a small bazaar – in other words, forming self-contained, semi-autonomous communities. It was only thus that a relatively frictionless community life could be assured to the various ethnic and religious groups. The towns had a public sector comprising the bazaars, caravanserais, mosques, schools (madrassas), mausoleums and public baths, and a private sector with the various dwellings which were as a rule only entered by those who lived in them. A third sector – that of the state or the ruler – was often strikingly manifested in the so-called 'ark', a fortified citadel dominating the town, and frequently built on artificial hills. This ark usually contained the court mosque, a prison, the state mint, and the barracks with arsenal and stables, as well as the ruler's palace. The 'registan', a large square where parades, riding exhibitions, markets and public executions were held (the court usually sat under the arch of the main entrance to the palace), often provided a transition zone between the state and the public

sector. The registan was surrounded by the most magnificent madrassas, caravanserais, guesthouses and an important mosque. The main entrance to the bazaar arcade was usually nearby.

Legally speaking, the towns were the property of the respective ruler, on whose goodwill depended the weal or woe of every single inhabitant. A sense of citizenship could not develop under such circumstances. There were no civil rights in the towns.

Most of the population consisted of poor dependent tradesmen as well as an army of court servants and the numerically small upper class. The work of these tradesmen was commissioned by a wholesale merchant who also leased them their workshops, supplied them with raw materials and marketed their products which, legally, were his property, on his own terms. The craftsmen often did not even own their tools. They were mostly too poor to use their own products. Independent craftsmen were extremely rare. This means that urban culture was enjoyed by and in the hands of an upper class consisting of about 5–10 per cent of the inhabitants – civil servants, military and religious functionaries, intellectuals (teachers at the madrassas), merchants and rich landowners who lived in the town on the yields produced by peasants who leased their estates. Since there were no civil rights, we cannot call this upper class an 'haute bourgeoisie', though they doubtlessly had a corresponding lifestyle. It is from these households that our material originates. Most town dwellers had so few possessions that they hardly differed from the dependent peasants or impoverished nomads. These possessions were so simple that they cannot be classified as belonging to any particular group or town. The most important items – cooking pots, jugs, crockery – were described when we presented the nomad's household effects.

Ill. 42 Imported Russian porcelain bowl (Kusnozeva) with repair work by a professional porcelain mender that is typical in Afghanistan. The repairs show how treasured imported porcelain was. D. 24.5 cm

*) The author has dealt elsewhere in greater detail with the subject of the 'oriental city' (Kalter, 1976). There is also a number of very interesting works by geographers and architects (among them Bianca, Wiche and Wirth).

Ill. 44 Detail of the door post in Ill. 43

The House

Even urban dwellings are made of loess clay, sometimes mixed with chaff, or constructed with unfired clay bricks, enclosed with a windowless wall on the side facing the street. The only variation in an otherwise quite monotonous prospect is provided by the relatively small doors decorated with carvings that are often reminiscent of Timurid ornamentation. There are far more one-storey than two-storey buildings. From the street it is impossible to tell whether one is standing in front of a poor man's or a wealthy man's house. In the centre of the house there was an open courtyard, in which wealthy people often laid out a garden with a fountain. Directly behind the entrance (often staggered to prevent people in the street from looking in), there was the men's section (selamlik) with the reception room for guests. In another wing of the building – in wealthy homes this was in a second inner courtyard which was separated by a wall with a narrow and low entrance – there was the women's section (haremlik) and the housekeeping rooms. In front of the reception room there is often a veranda which may be supported by columns which are mostly ornamented with carvings. The ornamentation, especially on the vase-shaped, narrowed base section of our column (very likely from Bukhara) (Ill. 43 and drawing) may be compared to columns preserved in public buildings from the Timurid or early Uzbek period (15th/16th century). Apart from the not very frequent but always high-quality carvings on wooden architectural elements, travellers in the 19th century describe the houses as unornamented. (The painstaking workmanship of the carvings is due to

Ill. 43 Carved door post of a town house, 19th c. 155 cm

Ill. 45 Teahouse in Samarkand, before 1890

Ill. 46   Sart kitchen, before 1890

the fact that in a country so poor in wood, it was considered an extremely valuable material.) Von Schwarz, who surely visited more houses than any other author during the fifteen years he spent in the country, reports, 'The interior and exterior walls of the houses as a rule are left as they are, and are therefore of the same yellowish-grey colour as the road pavement. . . Wealthy people, on the other hand, decorate the walls inside their homes with alabaster stucco work in Arabic style. Wall paintings are seldom found. These normally consist of arabesques in bright and crude colours, or of stylized flowers. . .'. The ceilings are usually made of tranverse beams embedded in the wall at 70 cm intervals, covered with reeds or twigs. The roof proper is made of compacted clay. Wealthy people often also decorate their ceilings 'most artistically, with highly convoluted and extremely complicated arabesques' (v. Schwarz). The houses of the poor had no windows at

all. In wealthy houses windows were placed above the door, and had wooden or stucco grids which could be glued over with parchment in winter as protection against the cold. Glass had not come to be commonly used even by the turn of the century.

The most detailed description of the furnishings is also given by von Schwarz. The following description is based on his report. In Turkestan houses (as elsewhere in the Orient) there was no heating. The wealthy made do with braziers in winter (Ill. 48). The clay floors were covered with reed mats or pieces of felt, the wealthy used carpets. There were neither chairs nor tables. One sat on the floor, or, if provided, on quilts filled with cotton, covered with printed fabric, ikat, or, more rarely, brocade. The use of tables and porcelain dishes (Ill. 9) only commenced under

Ill. 47   Door leaves of an Uzbek house in northern Afghanistan. The carved floral decoration in cartouches is very reminiscent of Moghul models. 175 by 76 cm

64

European influence. One normally ate from tin-plated copper trays which could be either round or oval (Ill. 46) set, where provided, on woven, embroidered or ikat cloths. Candelabra or oil lamps provided the illumination.

The only items of furniture – and even these only in the wealthiest homes – were bedsteads, consisting of a frame and feet made of round wood, spanned with a horsehair net, and cradles of the same type found everywhere from Turkey to Mongolia amongst all Turkish and Mongolian peoples. Cupboards are entirely lacking. In their stead, there were niches with shelves in the walls, which, according to von Schwarz, covered all four walls in the living room. 'These niches are either simple recesses. . . or artfully made compartments of alabaster. . . These niches serve to hang clothes and undergarments, and to store tableware, washing bowls, water and tea-pots, water-pipes, candelabra, fruit and food, perhaps books and the like.' 'To store their valuables, urban dwellers in Turkestan, like the nomads, use wooden chests reinforced with metal and painted green

or red, imported from Russia, and these are always one of the main decorative elements in the living room.'

Poplar chests decorated with metal, painting or chip carving are still made in northern Afghanistan today.

Our description may create the impression that urban dwellings made an extremely Spartan, drab impression. That this was not the case is due – as in the yurt – to the extremely variegated and colourful fabric furnishings, which, despite the outstanding quality of the items represented in collections gathered in the course of the last century*), were hardly noticed by either earlier travellers or even by von Schwarz.

The most important of these textile items were made by the women of the house and were an important part of the bridal trousseau. They are embroidered items for the most varied uses, usually known to us as 'susani' (needle-

Ill. 48   Cast iron charcoal holder, wicker for gathering camel dung, which is used as fuel, and fire fan. Measurements: d. holder 65 cm, d. basket: 63 cm, length of fan: 38.5 cm

work) (Ill. 59). They have become very well known during the past few years thanks to a number of exhibitions and related publications. We shall therefore confine ourselves to giving illustrations of two particularly characteristic pieces, though in our text at least, we want to present the most important forms and regional styles. An instructive and brief summary of the techniques used to make them and a description of their functions is given by F. Besch**).

The essence of what he says is given below:
1. Susanis served as wall drapings on feast days or as bedcovers for newlyweds. Their dimensions range from 230–280 cm by 170–200 cm.
2. Nim-susanis (semi-needlework) are much rarer. They are also used as wall hangings and are about half the size of susanis.

Ill. 49   Cast iron pots. The left-hand pot was made in northern Afghanistan, the right-hand one is a Russian import. 29 and 28.5 cm

3. A form designated takiapush, dzhoishab, polinpush or jasdigpush – also listed by Besch – is said to have been used as a curtain for niches. Neither the ornamentation nor the size, which Besch gives as 170–250 × 120–150 cm, are so strikingly different as to make it meaningful to classify this group as different from the susanis proper. We assume that susanis were also used as niche curtains.
4. 'Ruidzhos' (Tadzhik, meaning literally 'at the place') are large-sized cloths, with the mihrab-shaped (i. e. shaped like a prayer niche) inner area left unembroidered. They are said to have been used as the bed linen for newlyweds. This profanation of the mihrab form seems very unlikely to the author. It seems to me more likely that they were used as shrouds. (A reference to such a use of embroidered cloths 'mostly covered with large, red, stylized roses' is found in the writings of von Schweinitz.)
5. The designation 'dzhoi namas' (prayer embroidery), the mihrab décor and the format (130–150 × 90–110 cm) leave no doubt as to the use to which these cloths were put. They were used instead of a prayer rug for the devotions which every Moslem is required to perform five times a day.
6. Sandalipush are small, square cloths with embroidered edges and a central design, which were laid over a wooden frame on top of braziers. The hands were put under these cloths to warm up. (Cloths of this size are found everywhere in the Orient where braziers are used.)

Embroidered door-frames are also found, though rarely.

To date, I have come across only two very small, square cloths embroidered in typical susani style, which might have been bread cloths.

The cultivation and processing of cotton already had a long tradition by the 19th century. Unbleached cotton fabric was the most frequently used base for embroidery. One-colour silk fabrics were used only in rare cases. (Our collection includes one piece of susani embroidery on ikat fabric with a green background. Despite the outstanding craftsman – ship of both the embroidery and the ikat, this must have been too colourful even for the colour-loving inhabitants of Turkestan. I know of no other similar case.) Up to well into the eighties of the last century, cotton fabrics were woven in the home on narrow looms. The oldest known susanis are made of 5–6 strips each 25–30 cm wide. These strips were made one by one, sometimes embroidered by different women, and then sewn together. This is why the patterns are often not quite congruent. From the eighties on, wider

*) G. Rickmer's collection in the Western Asian Department of the Museum für Völkerkunde in the Stiftung Preussischer Kulturbesitz in Berlin and the Moser-Charlottenfels collection in the Historisches Museum, Berne.
**) In the catalogue: *Susani, Stickereien aus Mittelasien* * Copyright F. Bausback, Mannheim, 1981.

68

webs of material still with a relatively coarse structure were used, obtained from Turkestan weavers. These were replaced towards the end of the 19th century by pure white or one-colour (red, green, violet) cotton fabrics of fine weave, industrially produced in Russia.

The embroidery yarns used for earlier susanis were of locally produced silk, dyed by traditional methods. Von Schwarz reports that the dyes used were indigo imported from India, cochineal (a red dye obtained from the shield louse), imported from Russia, yellow obtained from a flower of the larkspur genus and from sophora Japonica, black from the peel of pomegranates and the galls of the pistachio tree. These early susanis can be recognized by the differences of shading in different batches of the same colour (when dyed with natural dyes, different batches never come out exactly the same shade) and by the variously bleached colours. Towards the end of the century, the use of aniline dyes spread with the importation of cotton fabrics. The more recent susanis are easy to recognize by their glaring colours. The tradition of making susanis has continued to the present day. Machine-embroidered susanis mark the end of this development.

Bukhara, Nurata, Karsh, Shahrisabs, Samarkand, Dzhizak, Ura-Tyube, Khodzhent, Pskent and Tashkent have been localized as the centres of susani production. We want to describe only three of these regional styles because these clearly show the markedly different influences under which they must have been created.

Although it may be assumed that the susani craft has a very old tradition, no pieces are known to originate with certainty prior to the middle of the last century. Besch believes that the precursors of susani ornamentation, which, with the dominance of its floral ornamentation clearly differs from the traditional ornamentation of the steppes, are to be found in Soghdian wall painting, but also draws attention to stylistic analogies in the miniatures and architectural ornamentation of the Timurid period.

The Bukhara susanis are almost always divided into a central section and a strikingly wide marginal strip, a main border. Between the main border and the central section and providing the outer boundary, there are subsidiary borders. This subdivision is reminiscent of a classical oriental carpet. The white background is embroidered with rosette-like red flowers with very different internal designs. These may alternate with bell-like flowers. The central section is frequently divided up into a network of rhombuses by jagged or lobed leaves. The rosettes may be accompanied by panicles. The dominant colours are red and green. (Ill. 59 shows a typical item of this type.) Especially the latticework in the central area reminds me of paintings in Moghul palaces.

Ill. 50 Woman and children from Bukhara, before 1890

This relationship to Moghul painting, as well as to well known works of semi-precious stones set in marble found in Moghul palaces and tombs (the Taj Mahal) is even more striking in the susanis from Nurata (Ill. 58).

The edging is not significantly different from Bukhara work. Flowering bushes or branches with a great many small red, yellow or blue single flowers, are strewn loosely in the central section. If one knew nothing of the background, especially of the embroidery technique, one would not hesitate to classify such a piece as belonging to a Moghul court. (In the abovementioned Bausback catalogue, p. 33, an item is even illustrated with a décor reminiscent of the layout of a Moghul garden.) The susanis of all other production centres (except Tashkent) are stylistically closely related to one of the two styles described above.

No satisfactory explanation has been found for the striking similarity of susani ornamentation to the Moghul tradition. As may be remembered, Babur, the founder of the Moghul Dynasty came from Turkestan. Does this striking similarity stem from the Timurid heritage of both cultures? Up to 1785, the crown prince of the Dzhanids ruling in Bukhara lived in Balkh. We know that a thin but uninterrupted stream of trade took place with India via Balkh. Are these similarities the result of the interchange of goods and ideas in the Uzbek Khanate period which is closer to us? But why, then, is the similarity greatest in Nurata, a small market town with a Tadzhik population some hundred kilometers to the north of Bukhara, and not in the capital city of Bukhara itself where there was still a small colony of Indian merchants in the 19th century?

In my opinion, the best known type of Tashkent susani belongs to an entirely different, pre-Islamic ornamental tradition. Red circles in the central area and borders cover the base almost completely. The pattern is called 'oi-paliak' (meaning 'moon sky'). The circles are surrounded by leafy creepers. In later pieces (from the turn of the century on), the creepers tend to disappear while the circular moons grow larger and larger.

In a recent Soviet publication *(Folk Art of Uzbekistan)*, it is pointed out that, as proved by archeological findings at various sites in Turkestan, printed fabrics have been manufactured since the fifth century AD. The ornamentation and colours of these printed fabrics used as bed sheets, table cloths and wall draperies, are reminiscent of similar red-grounded pieces from Isfahan and Yazd (Iran). On the other hand I was offered printed fabrics in Tashkurgan, which, according to some, were supposed to have come from Uzbekistan, while most informants maintained that these were formerly made in Tashkurgan (Ill. 156). The basic material consists of coarse strips of unbleached cotton, like the early susani. Dark brown and pale yellow appear as well as the main colour, red. Stylistically, there are relations to 18th/19th century northern Indian prints which adhere to

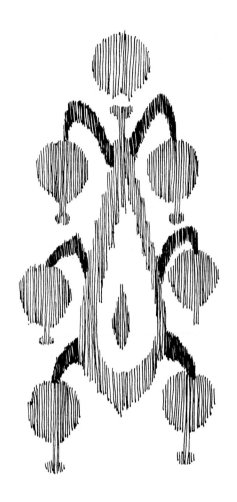

Ill. 51   Tree of life motif from an ikat cover, cypress with pomegranates

motifs such as combinations of stars and crosses (*see Folk Art of Uzbekistan,* Ill. 77), reminiscent of Seljuk tiling, realistic and abstract human figures and trees of life (Ill. 56 and Ill. 51). Despite the creditable work of the important researcher in the field of folk textiles, Alfred Bühler, and an article by A. Janata published in 1978, this fascinating field has barely been touched on in my opinion. The authoritative monograph on central Asian ikat still remains to be written. Bühler assumes – and this assumption is supported by Janata – that ikat was already produced in Turkestan in the eighth century AD. The immense number and variety of patterns used in ikat offer an as yet undeciphered pattern book on which the cultures with which Turkestan had contact (China, Tibet, India, Iran) may have left their mark.

The word 'ikat' originated in Indonesia. This method of fabric dyeing, like batik, is a so-called 'resist' or 'reserve' technique, and was developed to a high level of perfection there. According to the literature, in Turkestan, silk and mixed silk/cotton fabrics are called 'abra' or 'adra', in Afghanistan (according to Janata), generally 'pardah' (meaning a curtain).

To make ikat, the yarn is stretched on the loom. The work is described by Janata as follows: 'In the present case, the threads of the warp are dyed *before* weaving by tying them together in bundles according to the desired pattern. A material of several colours requires several binding and dyeing processes. Since it is impossible to tie the bundles so tightly that sharp outlines are produced, ikat weaves can be recognized by the way the coloured sections flow in the direction of the patterned threads. One ikat weave in Bukhara required the services of nine specialists, from spinning the silk yarn to weaving. In other places, for simpler fabrics, fewer sufficed.' It is not yet clear who made ikat fabrics. The repeatedly expressed theory that it was made by Jews has not been substantiated. Janata's conclusion that they were made by Tadzhiks is the most probable, especially since all the data relating to what craftsmen belonged to which ethnic groups, indicate most of the craftsmen practising technically sophisticated crafts were in fact Tadzhiks. The importance of ikat in urban culture has been described by B. Dupaigne as follows: 'Ikat fabrics are luxuries given as gifts of honour at weddings and on other important occasions. The wealth of a landlord or merchant is indicated by the richness and newness of his garb. The patterns change annually with the fashion.' Another resist technique is that of making patterns by tying up the finished fabric before dyeing it. This is practised but plays only a minor role in the manufacture of veils and lining materials.

Apart from metalware – to which we shall now turn – textiles were certainly the most important craft products in Turkestan towns. Together these two created a congenial atmosphere in otherwise simply furnished homes. Both

the Moghul tradition. The art of making printed fabrics must have declined in importance by the end of the last century both in Russian Turkestan and in Afghanistan on account of the importation of cheaper, more colourful Russian-made printed cloths.

Better represented in western collections is ikat, an outstanding product of Turkestan textile handicrafts. This was put to a variety of uses in Turkestan households as table cloths, niche curtains, tapestries, bedclothes, covers and cushion covers. It was, and still is, a popular material for making clothes.

Its extremely varied patterns range from simple stripes and zigzag patterns through curved lines, to hooks, 'cloud-band' and circular ornamentation (Ill. 56), classic Islamic

could easily be transported to the flat roof of the house where most evenings and nights were spent in summer, or to the yurt or the rectangular Bukhara tents with pyramid roof which wealthy townspeople still had in their garden in the 19th century and into which they moved in the summer.

After listing the scanty furniture, von Schwarz closes his description of the furnishings with the following list: 'The only other household effects found in addition to those already mentioned, in the homes of the sedentary inhabitants of Turkestan are their unique teapots and cups, washbowls, brass plates, waterpipes and bird cages.'

The Museum für Völkerkunde Berlin (Museum of Ethnology) has published an excellent work on the products of Turkestan metalworkers (S. Westphal-Hellbusch, I. Bruns, 1974). It is based on the Rickmer collection gathered in the nineties of the last century, which includes virtually all the important types of vessels. In this work, all accessible sources relating to metal craftsmen in the Bukhara bazaar, metalworkers and guilds, the organization of work, the division of labour, supplies of raw materials, alloys, the history of metalwork and traditional ornamentation, have been analysed and clearly presented. For the specially interested, this study is indispensable. We shall therefore keep our comments as brief as possible. Besides presenting the most important types of vessels, we shall give only the background information we consider to be absolutely essential. Unless otherwise stated, our information is based on the above-cited work (when dealing with the 19th century).

East Khorassan, to which part of Turkestan belongs, may be considered the place where the altogether unique Islamic style of metalwork originated (D. Barret, A. S. Melikian Chirvani). The author recently expressed the view (Kalter, 1982) that Turkish influence played a determining role at the very beginnings of this development in the 10th century – a thought already touched on in a more general form by Diez, 1915. Ornamental traditions may be traced right back to this early period and even earlier. Apart from exceptions – of which we shall consider one – in the 19th century we no longer find vessels with forms related to these early forms. In Iran, where much more is known about the history of art, and a great deal of dated or datable material is available, tinned, chased copper vessels, and to a lesser extent, brass vessels were found to have replaced the heavy cast bronze vessels at the beginning of the 15th century.*) In our opinion, it was the use of these much more malleable materials and the savings in the amounts used, which made possible the changeover to lighter, curvier forms and to production for sale at the market (i. e. without a specific order from a customer) – a change which took place everywhere in the 15th century. For Turkestan we lack the data to prove this theory. But

we may well assume that this technological development won through relatively fast, thanks to continuing, though mainly unfriendly, contacts with Iran. That the development into indisputably uniquely Turkestan shapes commenced with the beginning of Uzbek rule at the beginning of the 16th century, as Russian authors maintain, remains mere speculation in view of the sources at our disposal.

The situation in the 19th century was as follows: metal vessels were apparently made at all important Turkestan markets. In the Emirate of Bukhara, the city of Karshi was an important manufacturing centre as well as Bukhara itself. The extent of regular trade between the various manufacturing places within Turkestan is not clear. It is certain, however, that not all the pieces that came on the market in Bukhara were actually made in the city or in the Emirate of Bukhara and, vice versa, that metal products which had been acquired, though not necessarily made in Bukhara, were to be found everywhere in Turkestan. The function of Bukhara as a trading centre may be substantiated by the following quotation: 'Everything is produced by domestic industry and cheap, so that the Bukhara clothes market provides all True Believers well into eastern Turkestan with fashionable suits. The Kirghiz, the Kipchak and the Kalmuk is accustomed to making an excursion there from the desert. Here he finds what he considers the pinnacle of civilization. Bukhara is his Paris and London.' (von Hellwald, cited after Westphal-Hellbusch).

It has been difficult to ascertain to which ethnic group metal craftsmen belonged. Apart from the Tadzhiks, Iranian slaves are the most likely. The craftsmen seem to have been organized in guilds, althoug the question remains unanswered as to whether it was only the single specialists who were organized or all metalworkers. There were specialists (copper and brass smiths) who made the form, founders who made handles, the connecting pieces for the spouts and the decorative knobs for the lids, and artists who made the ornamentation by engraving or other techniques which will be described below. Often there were other specialists to solder the pieces together, to flange the bottom of the pieces and to rivet handles, lids and ornamental knobs. With copper vessels, finally, other specialists performed the tinning. In such cases, the décor was engraved after tinning in order to obtain as clear a contrast as possible. For the same reason, the background of brass vessels was sometimes blackened with asphalt, or treated with red, blue or green sealing wax. This last technique is widespread particularly in northern India. The practice of applying mirrors (Ill. 52), glass beads, brass on copper and vice versa, is also found (Ill. 60). The bottom part of a waterpipe on Ill. 60 lower left, is particularly interesting in

---

*) This development seems to have begun in the environs of Ghazni and Herat in the second half of the 12th century.

Ill. 52 Metalware from urban Turkestan households. Left: washing utensils consisting of washbasin and jug, Russian chased silver work presumably made as a present for the court at Bukhara. Right: washing utensils, brass with engraved décor, Bukhara. Centre: water pipe, brass with cast and engraved décor, and pieces of mirror glass; a wooden connecting piece between the lower part and the top is missing. Left, h. of jug: 26 cm, d. basin: 27 cm, centre, h: 55.5 cm, right, h. of pot: 31 cm, d. basin: 32.5 cm

this connection because besides specially made brass disks, others of specially cut old material were also applied – a procedure which is surprising in view of the otherwise very carefully crafted piece, but one which is also occasionally found in jewellery.

Turkestan's own well known abundant ore deposits were no longer worked in the 19th century. The raw material was mainly imported from Russia, copper was imported to a lesser extent from British India well into the eighties.

Ill. 52 shows the utensils which were absolutely essential for well-bred Turkestan hospitality. On the left and the right-hand sides there are washing sets consisting of a jug and a bowl with a removable, sieve-like insert. The set on

the right is supposed to come from Bukhara, the left is a skilfully made piece of chased silver and demonstrates the adaptability of Russian manufacturers in making items for fastidious customers as well as mass products. It bears a Russian stamp and was very likely made in the 19th century as a gift for a Turkestan nobleman or courtier of high standing. The item in the centre is a water pipe. A turned connecting piece between the lower section and the top may have been lost. The shape of the lower section is reminiscent of a calabash (gourd) which probably inspired the development of this form. In any case, there are water-pipes with a lower section consisting of a calabash in a metal mounting.

Water jugs, always recognizable by the spout which is frequently decorated with applied ornaments, are shown in Ill. 53. An interesting feature of the unusually large piece with relatively archaic-looking décor is the particularly clear water-dragon head at the top of the handle (see drawing 54) and the lion's head at the end of the spout.

Traditional teapots (kungans) are amongst the most original creations made by Turkestan craftsmen, and are

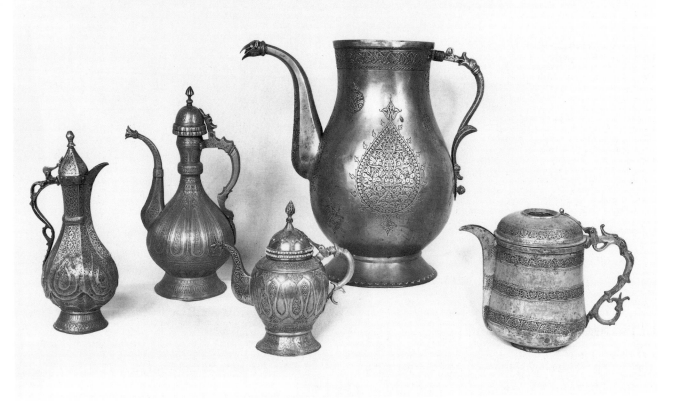

*Ill. 53   Teapots and water jugs, and to the right a samovar from Turkestan
towns. Jugs and pots of brass, the samovar of tinned copper. The engraved décor, especially of the two right-hand pieces, shows clear references to Timurid ornamental traditions, 19th c. H. from 21 to
40.5 cm*

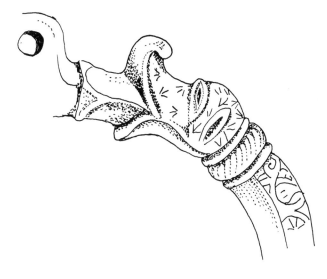

*Ill. 54   Cast dragon's head from the end of a jug handle. The shape is found
from Timurid times and is supposed to protect the contents of the
vessel from contamination*

Ill. 55 Heads of flowers, above, from the handle of a Moghul sword c. 1600, below, from a pouring vessel from Bukhara towards the end of the 19th c

recognizable by their typical spouts (Ill. 60 and Ill. 53). There are flattened oval shapes as well as the pear shapes shown here. The 'filta'-type teapot, shown in Ill. 60 on the right-hand side, is probably not very old, but in view of its clear shape which is reminiscent of the 'melon-domes' of Timurid architecture, and the absence of any engraved décor, it certainly goes back to a very early type. (Teapots with the same formal design are known from earlier Moghul material. Direct transmission of form and ornamentation appears to have existed also between Turkestan and Kashmir which were connected by a trade route. However, the Kashmir and Moghul Indian styles seem to have exerted a direct influence on each other.) In the centre of Ill. 53 there is a recent teapot shape which was probably made at the end of the last century in imitation of Russian porcelain teapots. In the 19th century samovars seem to have existed only as Russian imports. In any case, von Schwarz does not mention any samovars produced in Turkestan and none is included in the Rickmer collection. Accordingly their production must have only commenced after the turn of the century. It is therefore interesting to note that the specimen in Ill. 53, right, is decorated with an engraved lotus tendril of the type which, to our knowledge, first appeared in the Timurid period. Another large samovar has a bird decoration practically identical to the engraving on a late Ghaznevid kettle in the Linden Museum collection (Ill. 169).

By far the oldest vessel shape in the Linden Museum collection is shown in Ill. 14, right. This item is one of the few pieces from the Rickmer collection to reach the Linden Museum, and accordingly, must have been collected in Bukhara in the nineties. A piece with a similar shape was published by J. Kusmina in the *Afghanistan Journal* in 1980. This was found during excavations in northern Afghanistan and originates from the first centuries of the last millenium BC. From the Islamic period, there are pieces of similar shape, again for the Timurid period. Creeper ornamentation on the spout is also in the Timurid tradition. A creeper with five-petal blossoms turns into a forked-leaf creeper on the pointed spout – a change of motif which, to my knowledge, appeared for the first time during the Timurid period. The body of the vessel has a décor consisting of eight-pointed stars filled with three-part flowering bushes. This star/bushes pattern first appeared in Iran as far back as the late Seljuk period (end of the 12th/beginning of the 13th century). The most obvious parallels, however, are to be found in Moghul material.

Ill. 56 Examples of decorative silk ikat cloths, of the kind used as curtains and covers in Turkestan urban households. In order to give an idea of the great variety of ikat patterns, we have photographed details of four cloths side by side

Ill. 57   Example of the typical floral decoration of a susani from Samarkand

Towards the end of the 19th century, imported Russian cast-iron pots had become widespread everywhere although there were founders in Turkestan, too. A comparison of the imported cast-iron jug (Ill. 49) and one which was probably made in a workshop in northern Afghanistan (same illustration) gives an idea of how much poorer the quality of local cast-iron products was than that of imports.

An indirect proof of the decline in Turkestan cities is given by the vessel shown in Ill. 14 left. Both the form and the inscription*) indicate that this pot was used for sherbet (a lemonade-like refreshing beverage) which probably comes from a mosque. On feast-days the faithful were offered a refreshment. The condition of the vessel shows that it was used for cooking until very recently. The calligraphy and the ornamentation both suggest that it very likely originated in the 16th or 17th century.

Other household effects mentioned by von Schwarz include locally manufactured tea bowls made of clay – to our knowledge none have survived – and porcelain bowls and cups. The extent to which Russian exporters adapted to the newly developed market is demonstrated by the following inscription in Gardener bowls in the Museum's collection: 'Admirable is the bowl which contains such pleasurable things. It is handed around whenever friends meet. It was ordered by a merchant of Bukhara in 1328 (= 1910)'. Inscriptions were a popular decorative element on table ware. They also showed how far popular piety had permeated everyday life. A ceramic plate probably made at the end of the last century in Tashkurgan bears the following inscription: 'From the beginning, when He (Allah) made paradise, He determined fates. May he who eats palouv (Tadzhik for 'pilaf', a rice dish) from this plate eat his fill. Likewise may he who eats shurvah (soup) from this plate eat his fill.' Ceramic plates and bowls for food, in shapes and with glazings of a type already used in the 10th century (Ill. 8) were mainly used in poorer households. The metal plates, tins with lids and pots with handles known to the author (e. g. those published in the Berlin catalogue) do not markedly differ from Iranian pieces either in form or in ornamentation. At the present stage of research it is impossible to say whether the otherwise so creative Turkestan metal craftsmen here merely copied Iranian models, or whether the pieces were all imported from Iran or whether specialization amongst the metal craftsmen went so far as to

Ill. 58   Susani from Nurata. The embroidered décor in bright colours is reminiscent of paintings in Moghul palaces

---

*) The inscription reads: 'O thou the owner of this. . . May thy star stand high. I wish that thou shalt always be protected from the envious. So long as the (this?) heaven exists, this bowl shall always be full of sherbet and then again empty of sherbet.' My thanks to Mr Saeed Motamed, Frankfurt, for reading and translating this inscription.

77

Ill. 60   Metal vessels from urban Turkestan households, copper with engraved brass or embossed silver décor, brass with engraved and stamped décor; the centre jug has inlaid glass stones. From left to right: lower part of a water pipe, two wash jugs and two teapots. H: from 35 to 24 cm

Ill. 59   Decorative wall hanging, 'susani', Bukhara, probably before 1880. Base fabric, five strips of a coarse raw white cotton cloth woven at home, embroidered with silk. L: 244 cm, w: 152 cm

have this particular commodity manufactured only by Iranian slaves. The demand for such plates must have been tremendous. Von Schwarz describes a type of cold buffet known as a 'dostarkhan' served to guests as 'appetizers' which, depending on the social status of the host, consisted of 50 to 100 plates containing various breads, sweets and fruit.

It was not customary to use cutlery. One ate – as everywhere else in the Orient – with one's fingers. Soups were drunk. Simple wooden spoons (Ill. 40) existed, however.

Of the presumably numerous utensils used in the kitchens of the rich (ladles, perforated spoons, stirring spoons, spatulas, sieves, mortars) we know nothing. The mortars in Rickmer's collection are from the 12th/13th century, and are hardly likely to have still been in use. The reason for this is simple. The travellers and collectors of the last century were men. The kitchen was part of the women's province and, as such, was closed to them.

Turkestan Costume

Clothing and jewellery together make up the costume of mankind. For reasons of economy in this book we have refrained from describing them separately, because regional clothing customs which vary very little are opposed to a broad spectrum of the most varied forms of jewellery. In this survey, we shall try to contrast Turkmen and Uzbek clothing directly. The harsh life of the steppes meant that Turkmen male clothing was extremely simple, whereas in the cities a subtly graduated system governing the use of different valuable materials for men's coats grew up (Ills. 63, 64). The wearer's social status could be clearly judged from his coat, but also by the colour and size of his turban cloth. There was very little male jewellery as such. The male need for jewellery and display, both among Turkmen and in the towns, was expressed in the use of richly ornamented bridles, costly saddles and saddlecloths.

As no man would walk unless he was forced to, making the images of horse and rider virtually inseparable, it seems reasonable to treat the horses' trappings as an element of male dress. Ostentatious weapons undoubtedly formed one element of male dress. They, too, often provided pointers to the wearer's social status; for example, daggers, like the one shown in illustration 70, upper left, were bestowed as a sign of honour by the Emir in Bukhara. To sum up, we can say of male costume that the clothing of urban upper class men was much more costly and colourful than that of the Turkmen.

The picture was exactly the opposite in the case of female costume. The walking-out dress of urban women consisted of a ground-length sleeveless cotton robe. It was generally made of pale white-striped green, brown or dark blue cloth, with two long tapering pieces of material like dummy sleeves, sewn together and hanging down the back. This robe completely enveloped the woman. The face was covered with a dense horsehair or cotton veil (Ill. 114). Any jewellery worn was invisible. Turkmen women were unveiled – as were all female nomads. A coat similar to the robe described above (called kurthe, kurteh, charpy or chyrpy) was shorter; it barely covered the hips, was richly embroidered and had different colours depending on the age of the wearer. The wearer's outward appearance was decisively stamped by the lavish use of jewellery. Turkmen wo-

men's dress and jewellery were essentially richer and more differentiated than those of their urban counterparts.

That diagnosis is applicable to the whole of the Islamic world. At one time it was certainly connected with the absence of compulsory veiling in the case of nomad women – what was the point of urban woman owning large quantities of jewellery which no one saw except her husband and her sons? – but also with the generally stronger position of the

Next two pages

Ill. 63   Turkestan men's coats.Top: two silk ikat coats with silk linings, Samarkand, first third of the 20th c. Bottom left: coat of a dignitary, imported Russian gold brocade, silk ikat lining, Bukhara? end of 19th c. Bottom right: cotton coat with white cotton lining and narrow ikat stripes on the front seams. Striped cotton fabrics are preferred by Turkmen, but are also worn by all the other groups. Northern Afghanistan, 20th c.

Ill. 64   Velvet ikat coat of a dignitary from Khiva with embroidered cuffs and Russian printed cotton material as a lining. End of 19th c.

Ill. 61   Wife of a Teke Khan, before 1890

Ill. 62   Urban woman's coat, part of the walking out dress worn pulled over the head. The long dummy sleeves hanging down the back are characteristic. Green and white-striped cotton, silk lined. Mazar-e-Sharif, North Afghanistan, c. 1960

woman as the person mainly responsible for the herds in the nomadic economic system. But lastly – and this cannot be overemphasised – the abundance of Turkmen jewellery was probably occasioned by the need to insure against the risks of a nomadic economy by the possession of readily saleable, valuable and easily transportable reserves of capital.

Two quotations furnish impressive proof of this. As early as 1825, J. Fraser (cited in König) wrote: 'they do not . . . hoard their money; they most commonly turn it into such property as . . . women's ornaments.' (In those days they would not have possessed any money as such, apart from coins which were used as jewellery or converted into jewellery.)

The French nobleman H. de Blocqueville, who was a prisoner of the Turkmen from 1860 to 1861, supports this statement: 'One often sees repellently dirty women dressed in rags. They have only a small sack of corn to feed their family on and nothing to cover themselves with at night; but they are laden with jewellery which they do not take off even when sleeping and which they will only pawn as a last resort when their husbands force them to.' The need to pursue the 'accumulation of wealth' in the form of jewellery did not arise in urban cultures. The acquisition of property or participation in promising commercial ventures was always more attractive to the wealthy city dweller.

However, when making these statements we are not claiming that jewellery was of no significance in urban cultures. It will become apparent that the jewellers of Turkestan towns made very delicate jewellery, but its role must have been similar to the one it plays in our own culture. To the Turkmen jewellery was 'life insurance'; to the city dweller it was merely one desirable luxury and display article among others. Allied to frequently similar basic forms or at least comparable usage (e. g. diadems, Ill. 71; plait jewellery, Ill. 96; triangular amulets, Ill. 121), striking features of Turkmen items of jewellery – the earlier they are the more clearly this appears – are their clear form and ornaments and firstclass materials. These combine to give them a formal severity which the nomads' knotted products also exhibit. Urban jewellery – especially Khiva pieces which originated in the immediate vicinity of the Turkmen – makes a baroque and extremely colourful, but, in spite of the tremendous expenditure of labour, mostly a somewhat tinny impression. It is easy to imagine it next to the equally 'baroque' urban embroideries.

Male Costume

Schwarz writes about urban clothing: 'The outer garments of the Sarts, both rich and poor, are all made to one cut and one pattern, regardless of the figure and size of the man for whom the clothes are intended. For they are not made to order, but bought readymade in the bazaar as required.' Another peculiarity of the garments pointed out by Schwarz is that they have no pockets. This has two consequences. The first is that the personal effects that every man carries, such as toilet accessories (consisting of nail-cleaners, earspoons and often tweezers, (Ill. 65), chewing-tobacco holders (gourds with silver mountings or gourd-shaped silver holders), firelighters, small embroidered bags, etc. (Ill. 66), are worn attached to the belt. This applies to both urban and rural clothing. The second is that bags were replaced by much smaller, usually rectangular, embroidered pouches. The style of embroidery corresponds to the style of embroidery peculiar to the group.

Depending on the measurements of the wearer, the clothing consists of baggy knee-length or ankle-length trousers, held up by a tubular belt, and a collarless thigh-length shirt with a slit offset to the right. In sophisticated towns, both are made of white cotton; among simple people, farmers, and nomads of closely striped coloured fabrics. The winter version may be quilted with cotton stuffing. Wealthy townsmen owned similarly or even more widely cut yellow buckskin riding breeches, which were decorated with embroidery in the style of susanis (unfortunately this type is not represented in the Linden Museum collection). Over these they wore one or more widely cut ground-length cloaks called chapans with very broad sleeves, set exactly straight, which are usually so long that they cover the hands. If a man wears several chapans, the innermost one is belted. The belts of the wealthy may be made of embroidered cotton or leather and fastened with silver clasps, or the belt fastenings may be of metal (iron, brass, silver) with cut or open decor. Two-part belt fasteners with enamelling or niello décor are known from Bukhara. This kind of belt, which was worn by only the wealthiest men, was often further decorated with round sewn-on disks fashioned by the same technique. The simple people, farmers and nomads, held their chapans together, if they did so at all, with scarf-like cotton belts. Footware consisted of slippers of the type found throughout the East, shoes with high platform heels (men and women had the same shape) and, for riding, topboots with high heels shod with iron. Leather socks were worn inside slippers or shoes. The socks might be richly embroidered, like examples from Uzbek women in the environs of Tashkurgan. As already mentioned, the material used for the chapan varied considerably according to rank. Schwarz writes that the most sought after were made of cashmere. On the other hand, he illustrates several emirs and khans in velvet chapans with silver relief embroidery. Gold brocade coats, often like our example in Ill. 63 with silk ikat lining, or velvet ikat coats, Ill. 64, were reserved for princes or high court officials. The wide embroidered sleeves of our velvet ikat coat are unusual. The everyday wear of these dignitaries and ceremonial dress for the remaining members of the upper classes was the silk or semi-silk ikat coat (Ill. 63). The common people, farmers and Turkmen wore cotton chapans, as already mentioned. These were generally striped.

The only noticeable difference between Turkmen and town-dwellers was in their headgear. The large sheepskin hats of the Turkmen can be characterised as the sign of male tribal dress. Town-dwellers wore small, round, often richly embroidered caps at home or at work. When they went outside, these caps were enfolded in a turban. The quality of the little caps alone indicated the status of the wearer. The rich wore gold, silver or silk embroideries, which might be fur-lined. Simple little caps were of ikat or cotton, sometimes quilted and padded with cotton (Ill. 76). The fact that the shops of the cap-sellers were situated in the best positions in the centre of the bazaar shows the importance attached to them. In former times, the pattern on the little caps must surely have given information about the wearer's origin. But regional classifications are definitely no longer possible, especially as the patterns are subject to changes in fashion, according to my observations in northern Afghanistan*). The quality of the turban material also differed according to status. Schwarz says that gold embroidered cashmere turban cloth was reserved for the khans, while princes could wear gold brocade. Members of the upper classes wore white turbans, the cloth for which was imported from India or England; the people wore colourful cotton cloth. (Even today this holds good in northern Afghanistan.) Good turban cloth is still exported from India and Pakistan to northern Afghanistan.

Ill. 65 Items for the personal use of Turkestan men. Left: honing steel, below: urban flint steel, above: flint steel on leather pouch for holding flints and tinter, Ersari. Honing steel: 20 cm, flint steel: 13 cm, pouch: 14 cm

Ill. 66 Items for the personal use of Turkestan men. Silver. Left: toilet article with ear spoon and nailcleaner, Cornelians, Ersari. Next to them: toilet article with nailcleaner, tweezers and earspoon, silver, glass beads, rural Uzbek, northern Afghanistan. Right: tobacco containers, silver, partially fire gilded, Teke; gourds with silver mounting, Saryq or Ersari. Length from 9.5 to 20 cm

*) S. Westphal-Hellbusch has published the caps in the Rickmer collection of the Berliner Museum für Völkerkunde and gives a good idea of the wide variety, colour range and rich ornamentation of this mostly hidden item of clothing.

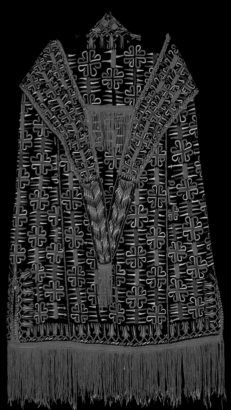

Horse Trappings

Given the frequently emphasised love the Turkmen feel for their horses, and the importance of jewellery in Turkmen culture, it is not surprising that anyone who could possibly do so adorned his horse as richly as possible. Vambéry used to make fun of the strange appearance of the poor ragged figures on their beautifully turned out horses. The bridles were set with rectangular or scoopshaped small silver elements, or round ones like upholstery nails. The adornment consisted of the head piece and a very wide neckpiece made of many leather strips set with silver (Ill. 5). In addition there might be two ornamental neck bands serving no practical purpose. A decorative breast band lay loosely on the shoulders just in front of the saddle or could be hung from the pommel; from its mostly dome-shaped, sometimes chased, centre a leather strap led to the girth, which as Ill. 26 clearly shows ran over the saddle. Cruppers were not necessarily used when riding on the

plains and as a result are generally absent. In recent years Turkmen horse ornamentation has come on the market in large quantities. The style of the silverwork corresponds to that of the other items of jewellery of the respective sub-tribe. Teke pieces are partially fire gilded (v. Technology of metalwork, p. 140) and Ersari pieces are pure silver, both being set with cornelians, the Turkmen's favourite stone. The author does not know of any horse decoration that can be classified as Yomut.

Urban horse decoration is much rarer in western collections and was less unified in style. Some princes did own gilded silver head pieces set with precious stones (rubies, etc). There is a type from Bukhara which was closely set with small turquoises. Our example, probably from Khiva, (Ill. 5) is covered with fire gilded silver fittings and is set with turquoises and cornelians. A velvet band serves as a rein. A striking feature of the neck adornment is the yak-hair whisk – a kind of horse ornament already known from Soghdian palace wall paintings in pre-Islamic times.

Previous two pages

Ill. 67   Women's mantles which are pulled over the head and serve as veils. Cotton with silk embroidery. The mantles form part of the costume of married women. The mantles of young women have a black ground, of middleaged women a yellow ground and of women over sixty a white ground. The rear side shows the dummy sleeves which are typical of Turkestan women's costume. Teke Turkmen. The mantle with a white ground may possibly still be 19th c.

Ill. 68   Teke woman's mantle. A mixture of cotton and silk, with partially fire gilded silver ornaments set with cornelians. Lining of Russian printed cotton. End of 19th c.?

Ill. 69   Turkmen weapons: two daggers with gold damascening or cut steel décor (cf. detail, Ill. 135), Walrus-ivory hilt and silverclad fire gilded sheath. The daggers are most probably 18th-c. Iranian urban work. The sheaths were obviously made for Turkmen. The left-hand one matches the style of Teke decoration, the second could be made for the Chaudors. Sabre, hilt set with cornelians, sheath with chip carving décor and leather, silver ornamented cover, Ersari. Length of daggers: 41 cm, 47 cm, length of sabre: 90 cm

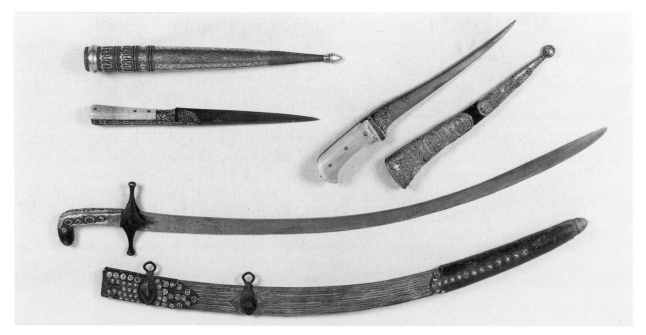

The shape of the saddle is the same for all Turkestan peoples. 'The saddle is usually carved from a single piece of wood. It is so arranged that only the stirrups lie on the horse's flanks, leaving its spine completely free.' (Schwarz.) Attached to the rear third of the bars are iron rings which are used to secure the baggage. With the help of the high forward saddlebow which terminates in a horn, tethering the animals in the country is avoided. The rein is tied round the horn. The horse's head is thereby drawn so far back that it cannot move and stands still for hours (Schwarz). The saddle decor consists of painting and engraved bone inlays at the edges (Ill. 5). Saddles were often used without padding by the nomads; townsmen always used them with cushions stuffed with cotton. Turkmen and Uzbeks used knotted saddle covers. As a support for the saddle they used fur, felt or also – among the wealthy – trapezoid saddlecloths with silver or gold relief, or silk embroidery, mainly on a red ground (Ill. 5). The saddlecloths were also sometimes laid over the saddle. Instead of

the saddlecloths of the townsmen, the Turkmen often used rectangular kelim cloths, which might be upholstered with horsehair, or, more rarely, knotted covers under the saddle. The front ends terminated in wide bands which could be closed in front of the horse's breast or sewn together at the front edges. The cover was pulled over the horse's head, falling into the right position in relation to the saddle. Felt covers with cloth appliqué work covering the whole horse were found only among the nomads. They had a hole for the pommel and so could be used while riding, if necessary. Von Schwarz claims that the Turkmen left their horses covered with these heavy felt trappings winter and summer. A leather whip, often with a silvercoated handle, completed the rider's equipment.

Weapons

The most important ceremonial weapon was the dagger, which the elegant man stuck in his belt. Daggers were housed in silver or silvercoated, or, among the Turkmen, partially fire gilded sheaths. The blades might be inlaid with gold ornamented with steel engraving decor (v. metal technology) on the base, the rear third of the back and the upper side of the tongue. Our two Turkmen daggers (Ill. 69) have walrusbone hilts which are riveted to the tongue. The hilt of our Ersari sabre (same Ill.) is set with silver fittings and cornelians. The wooden sheath adorned with simple chip carvings has a silverclad leather cover at its base

Ill. 70   Turkestan weapons; above left: dagger with damascened blade, horn hilt and silverclad, fire gilded sheath with chased décor and ornamental and glass stones on hilt and sheath, Bukhara, 19th c. Above right: dagger, damascened blade inlaid with gold on the upper part. Hilt with niello décor. Below: sabre, hilt with cut steel décor, leather covered sheath with silver fittings, urban weapon from north Afghanistan and yataghan-like sabre with horn hilt and gold damascened blade, possibly Bukhara, 19th c. Length of daggers c. 50 cm, length of sabre c. 95 cm

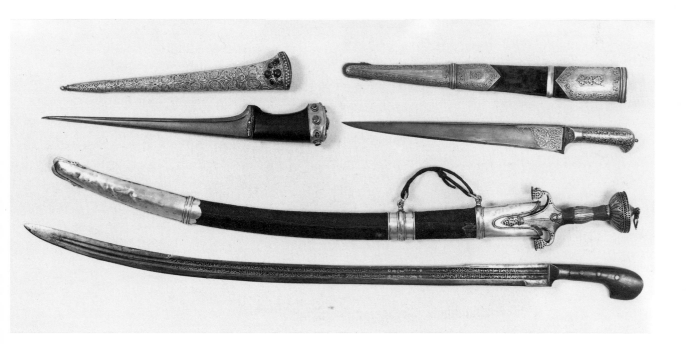

and tip. Ill. 70. shows urban weapons from northern Afghanistan and Russian Turkestan. The dagger (above left) was conferred as a token of honour. The damask blade*), at first glance entirely unornamented, reveals its true worth on closer examination. The gilded silver covering of the sheath is chased (detail, Ill. 131). Especially noteworthy on the right-hand dagger are the gold overlay at the base of the blade (detail, Ill. 137) and the niello work on the hilt, a technique that most probably came to Turkestan from the Caucasus. The floral decoration of the sheath is engraved and stamped. The sabre with the silverclad sheath comes from northern Afghanistan. The shape of its hilt resembles that of Indian weapons of the period. The hilt of the second sabre, shown without its sheath, with an extensive gold damascene inscription is characteristic of Caucasian weapons, but also occurred among 'Sart' weapons, according to Von Schwarz. The sabre is supposed to have come from Bukhara. So far the reference can only be guessed at, but both weapons and ornaments make us think of the influence, at least, of Bukhara craftsmen from the Caucasus. So much for the weapons which also had a ceremonial character. According to H. de Blocqueville, lances were still in use among the Turkmen around 1860. Von Schwarz, who wrote thirty-five years later, no longer mentions them. Firearms were apparently first introduced into Turkestan in large numbers in the second half of the last century. The first native gunsmiths started work in the 80s. Even then only the wealthiest Turkmen owned fork muskets. It cannot be determined whether battleaxes, as illustrated by Moser and Von Schwarz – they resemble an Iranian type – were still used or were purely display and ceremonial pieces.

---

*) Damask is a weld steel: this is a technical smithing product, originating from the interwelding and faggoting or bundling of iron and/or steel. (Hirschberg/Janata). The process is repeated several times. In comparison with the original material, the end product gains in hardness and elasticity. The complicated structure of damask steel can be made visible on the surface by chemical treatment.

Female Costume

The house dress of Turkestan women basically consists of trousers and a loose ankle-length dress fastened at the neck with a stud (Ill. 83, left) among the Yomut (sometimes also among Teke Turkmen women), but otherwise with ribbons. The clothing consists of silk or semi-silk fabrics. The favourite colour for Turkmen clothes is red with a yellow stripe, but violet is frequently used, too. The front of Turkmen dresses may be set from shoulder to waist with as many as a hundred silver pendants the size of a five-penny piece (Ills. 1, 61, examples of the pendants, Ill. 72). The ends of the trouser legs of Turkmen women may be completely covered with a wide piece of embroidery (Ill. 86), especially typical of the Ersari in northern Afghanistan. Yomut embroidery on dresses and trousers does not cover the whole background and has much less striking patterns. The favourite material for the shirts and trousers of urban women was ikat (Ills. 56 and 73). Ikat clothes have virtually become the national costume of Uzbekistan, but are frequently worn by Turkmen women. Instead of ikat clothes, wealthy women wore dresses of imported brocade or Chinese damask; poorer women wore monochromatic cotton dresses. Dresses made of Russian printed material with large flower patterns were and are worn by all Turkestan women.

The walking-out dress of urban women and female footwear have been described in the introduction to this chapter. We have also mentioned the corresponding item of clothing of Turkmen women, the chyrpy of Teke women covering the head and reaching to the hips. It was part of the dress of married women. According to Beresneva, young women wore chyrpys with a dark blue ground, while middle-aged women wore ones with a yellow and old women ones with a white ground. Dark blue chyrpys are usually the most lavishly embroidered, white ones, the most sparsely. Favourite motifs are flowering shrubs in the form

Ill. 71   Frontlets and diadems from Turkestan. Top: Silk embroidery on cotton, silver, partially fire gilded. Coral, turquoises and glass beads in the style of the Lakai Uzbek. Centre: partially fire gilded silver with cornelians, Teke. Bottom: silver with cornelians, Ersari. Width: from 35 to 54 cm

Ill. 72   Studs and pendants which are sewn on to clothing at breast height. D.: from 2.5 to 4.3 cm

Ill. 73 Sart woman, before 1890

a round cap, which may be topped by a dome-shaped silver element and is usually set with smaller silver components stamped in matrices. A narrow 'chain diadem' may also be sewn on. Braid jewellery may also be attached to the sides. Similar caps form part of the dress of rural Uzbek girls (Ill. 77).

Our qualifying remarks about the headgear of married women apply equally to jewellery. The debate about whether specific pieces of jewellery are head or neck, dorsal or pectoral adornments, is quite lively. For each item of jewellery there is undoubtedly a preference as to the way it is worn, just as certain pieces are normally worn in pairs. We shall present the usual way of wearing, disregarding some established exceptions. Why should not a piece worn on the head be worn round the neck for a change, or a dorsal ornament on the breast or an item normally worn in pairs be worn singly? It is equally possible that in Iran, where Teke and Yomut are intermingled, a women may wear Teke and Yomut pieces side by side. A Turkmen woman has no choice about wearing a maxi, middy or mini-skirt, but she has a certain freedom about choosing her jewellery and the way she wears it, even if that upsets our systematic minds. Turkmen women's dress lays strong emphasis on headgear. We shall return to the different forms in our detailed treatment of jewellery.

Turkmen women sometimes wore a coat over their dress. Our example (Ill. 68) comes from the Teke. It is lavishly adorned with jewellery and is closed with the typical rhomboid plates equipped with hooks and eyes (cf. also Ill. 80). The Yomut preferred wine-red or green velvet coats. The museum possesses an Ersari coat of violet silk. Urban women's coats worn at home or under their walking-out dress corresponded in cut – apart from minor variations – to the neck scallop of men's coats (Ill. 63), both according to the older literature and to illustrations. The comparatively short ikat coats with slit sleeves tapering towards the wrists and darts below the chest that have often come on the market in the last few years appear to be a recent development.

Turkmen belts like our example (Ill. 80) are extremely rare. Beresneva says they are used by both men and women, but they were definitely not a normal item of dress. In the towns, wearing belts was a masculine privilege.

of trees of life (Ills. 6 and 74). Individual flower stalks or shrubs or – more rarely – rhomboid lattices with a floral or palmleaf-like filling also occur. Among the floral motifs tulips and compositae shapes predominate. In striking contrast to the otherwise floral ornamentation is the richly varied décor on the tapering ends of dummy sleeves and on the front yoke, like a shawl collar, which often terminates in a rhomboid motif enclosed by rams' horns. In other Turkmen groups the chyrpy was replaced by a headcloth, generally red, which can, but does not have to, be pulled over a foundation of leather, plaited plant fibres, felt, or recently, board, or a high cap. There are obviously tribal and regional preferences involved; but equally obviously there are no rules without an exception. In general, we can only say that married women wear a headdress which covers the head, leaving only the ends of several pigtails which hang down the back visible. In the presence of strange men, young women in northern Afghanistan or Iranian Turkmen territory will draw part of the veil or chyrpy across their mouths. The unmarried girl, on the other hand, wears only

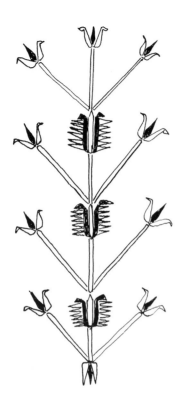

Ill. 74   Embroidered décor from women's coats. Above a stylised tree of life, below drawings of individual blooms (tulips and Compositae)

Ill. 75   Sart woman, before 1890

Next two pages

Ill. 76   Top: Turkmen caps. The three big caps were worn by the girls of North Afghan groups. In the centre of the picture, a boy's cap. which could come from the Yomut, judging by the style of embroidery. All 20th c. Bottom: Men's caps from Turkestan towns. The left-hand cap was made in Tashkurgan at the 60s or beginning of the 70s; the right-hand one was woven there in 1978. The cap with gold relief embroidery comes from Samarkand and was bought before 1920; the cap with the tree of life motif abstracted to a shrub with three flowers in the centre could have been made in Bukhara around the turn of the century

Ill. 77   Caps of marriageable girls from northern Afghanistan. The style of embroidery on the left-hand cap is typical of northern Afghan Turkmen. The additional ornaments show elements of the Teke style (crowning piece) and the Ersari style (plait jewellery). The right-hand cap shows both in the style of embroidery and in ornamental additions (with the exception of fire gilded parts, which point to Khiva) elements of typical Lakai Uzbek works

93

Children's Dress

The clothing of both sexes matched adult clothing in cut and material. As headgear they wore small caps (Ill. 76) which could be adorned with silver elements. There are special shapes of amulets for boys. Small round flattened cans were sewn on to children's clothing at shoulderblade height. There are dorsal amulets reserved for boys in the shape of a bow strung with an arrow, often treated so ornamentally that it becomes unrecognisable. Our Teke amulet (Ill. 78), bottom, is a very clear example. Rectangular amulets with two animal claws or silver imitations of claws are also sewn on to the backs of boys' shirts. Boys are obviously considered as particularly vulnerable. A peculiarity of children's clothing – apparently mainly of north Afghan Turkmen groups – is embroidered bibs (Ill. 85). The frequently sewn on triangles and rhomboids also have significance as amulets.

Women's Jewellery

In the introduction to this chapter we frequently mentioned women's jewellery, referring to its stylistic peculiarities and economic importance. Two quotations will serve to emphasise how large the amount of jewellery owned by Turkmen must have been: 'Their combined jewellery could reach a weight of 6–8 kg. Mrs Wasiljewa, the foremost expert on Turkmen jewellery remarks that the marriageable maidens and young women of rich families wore so much jewellery that they could only walk with difficulty.' D. Dupaigne (1978) even states that bridal jewellery weighed as much as 17 kg.

Ill. 78   Bow-shaped dorsal amulets for Turkmen boys. Above in the Yomut style. Below in the Teke style. The strung arrow can be easily seen in the lower piece. H.: c. 17 cm. w.: from 15 to 19 cm

Ill. 79   Floral motifs from Ghaznevid stone relief, 12th c., and an item of Turkmen jewellery Teke, 19th c

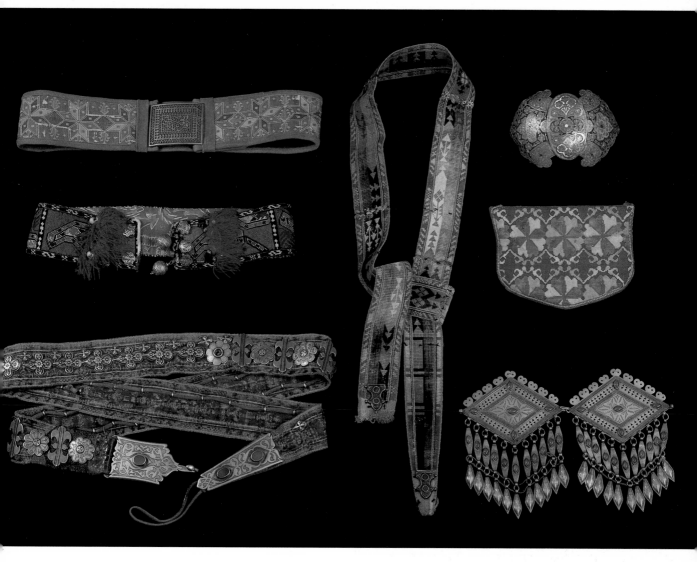

The enormous financial importance of Turkmen jewellery alone would call for intensive study by scholars. We know from other better researched fields of jewellery that forms of jewellery and ornaments were handed down for thousands of years. Whether permanence of form always implies permanence of meaning must obviously remain an open question, but we may assume it was so in many cases. We already have some clues to the longevity of the ornamental tradition of Eurasian steppe nomads. Thus frontal ornamental plates, which resemble in form the 'egmeh' of married Teke Turkmen women, were found in the some 2,400 year-old graves of Scythian women (illustrated in Trippett, p. 22). Other examples point in the direction of ancient Iranian traditions of jewellery. The applied embos-

Ill. 80 Belts, dress fastenings and belt pouch. Upper left: leather with silk embroidery, brass fastening with open work décor, Lakai. Centre: belt, cotton with silk embroidery and silver appliqué work, wrap fastening, urban work from Russian Turkestan. Below: belt, velvet band, silver appliqué work on leather mounting, partially fire gilded and set with cornelians. Fastened by a leather noose in the hook, long enough to be wrapped round the wearer's body more than once, Teke, 19th c. Belt closed by tying, velvet with silver appliqué. Above right: Two-part fastening, silver with émail champlevé, Bukhara. Centre: belt pouch, leather with silk embroidery, Bukhara? Two-part dress fastening for women's coats. Silver, fire gilded with cornelians, Teke. Wearing a belt was the privilege of upper class men in Central Asian towns. The common man held his coat together by tying a piece of cloth round it.

sed silver disks on our Teke coat (Ill. 68) have their counterpart in tombs of the east Iranian Dalaiman culture c. 1000 BC. Lastly, scholars have sweated blood and covered reams of paper in their attempts to interpret the rich ornamentation of Turkmen carpets and kelims. But hardly anyone has taken the trouble to compare carpet and textile ornamentation with jewellery décor, although there are numerous points of contact and overlappings which are often only confused by apparent differences really caused by the materials used. Like its ornamental tradition, the rich and varied Turkmen amulet tradition definitely conceals many references to the pre-Islamic shamanistic world picture, which could only be explained by intensive study of still intact shamanistic traditions. Here only the collaboration of archaeologists, prehistorians, historians and religious scholars, or at least the use of their methods, can improve our knowledge. In order to interpret plant or animal representations correctly, it may be necessary to consult botanists or zoologists specialising in the region concerned. There will inevitably be disappointments. Ultimately the answer to many questions must be wide of the mark. Every answer that is found throws up new questions. Preoccupation with such question posing may seem to be a hobby for ivory-tower scholars. It is far from this in my opinion. An interest in jewellery, which is so close to the wearer, leads, in such a jewellery-rich culture, to the solution of central problems such as the ethnogenesis, history and traditional religious thinking of the group and is therefore a necessary contribution to the understanding of that culture.

This digression is meant to draw attention to the importance of the subject of jewellery and may spur some of my readers to go into it in more detail. Within the framework of an attempt at a general summary of Turkestan culture, we can only extract the most important types of jewellery, pick out the characteristics of the best known substyles and transmit the little information we have about raw materials and craftsmen. (Technology is dealt with in a separate chapter.)

Ill. 81 Ersari Turkmen temple jewellery, silver with cornelians. 61.5 cm

Ill. 82 Yomut Turkmen jewellery. Silver with fire gilded appliqué, glass stones and cornelians. Left: collar studs. Centre: pectoral jewellery. Right: written amulet holder. D. of studs: from 9.2 to 13.6 cm, length of pectoral item: 53 cm, length of amulet holder: 67 cm

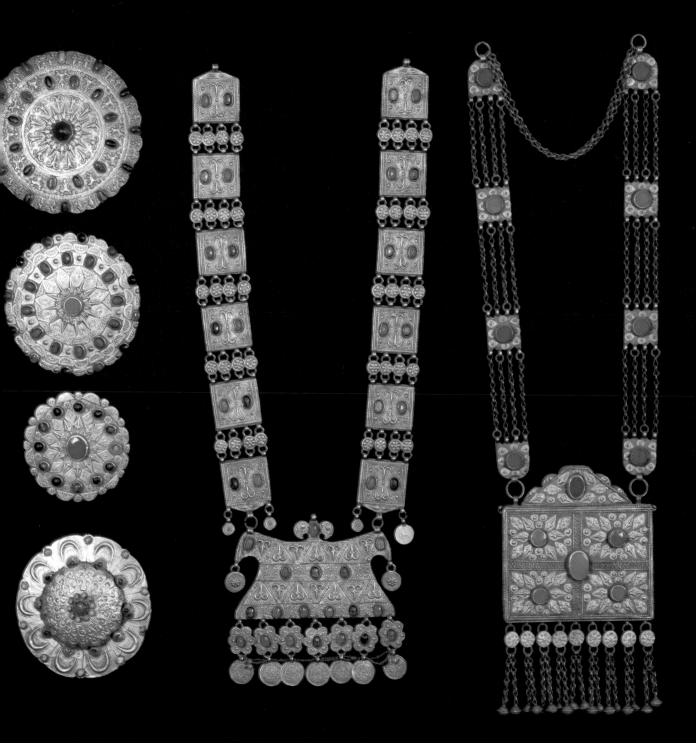

Ill. 83 Heart-shaped ornamental dorsal plates from different Turkmen groups. All of them silver with cornelians, above left without gilding, Saryk. Right: only the cross-shaped ornament terminating in trefoils is gilded, sub-tribe? Bottom left and centre: Teke; on the left-hand example the representations of riders on either side of the central cornelian are noteworthy (cf. Ill. 186), bottom right: Yomut heart. H. from 19.5 to 25.5 cm

Ill. 84 Iranian Turkmen necklets. Left: twisted silver band with cornelians; the ornamental plate in front is set with fire gilded appliqué, cornelians and glass stones, Yomut. Right: Horseshoe-shaped necklet, silver with simple engraved décor and cornelians, plate with appliqué chased in bottom swages and cornelian. Qara-dashly? From left to right: D.: 16.5 cm and 18.5 cm

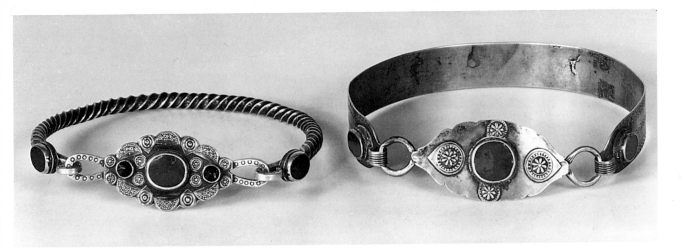

Ten years ago there was only scattered information on the subject of Turkmen jewellery. Since then, a series of publications of widely differing quality have appeared*. Our information about urban jewellery, which is much rarer in western collections and certainly played a lesser role in the culture itself (see above), is much scantier. My expositions on the theme are mainly based on the omnibus volume *Folk Art of Uzbekistan*, a Russian article**) and A. Janata, 1981, as well as my knowledge of some private collections and oral communications from my colleagues Böhning and Janata.

---

*) The most important are: L. Beresneva, 1976; J. A. Firouz, 1978; A. Janata, 1981 and J. Prokot, 1981.
In the autumn of 1984 a comprehensive publication of Turkmen jewellery will appear with the following title: Rudolph, Hermann: Der Turkmenenschmuck. Sammlung Kurt Gull. (Edition Hansjörg Mayer, Stuttgart, London.)

**) L. A. Tschjyri, 1977.

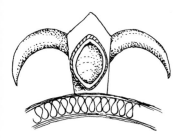
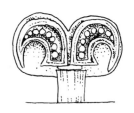

Ill. 85a Representations of ram's horns forming the terminal points of pieces of Turkmen jewellery

The Styles of Turkmen Jewellery

'Works on the problem of the stylistic provinces of Turkmen jewellery by Soviet ethnologists are not yet complete, let alone published. By and large, some provinces, which mainly coincide with the big tribes, can be traced.' (Janata, 1981).

When one says Turkmen jewellery, one generally refers to Teke jewellery. Its characteristic is the partial fire gilding of the ground and the lavish use of cornelians or glass beads of the same colour. Ornamentation is dominated by the fork-leaved runner which, powerfully or even sometimes crudely executed (e. g. Ill. 108, left), may stand free on a pure silver background. It may also be combined into candelabra-like structures to fill in wedges or triangles (Ill. 92). These inevitably invite comparison with 12th-century Ghaznevid stone reliefs (Ill. 12). Interweaving to form runners (Ills. 103 and 160), a feature which we already know from Timurid metal vessels, is also common. In addition to the runners, we find trefoil motifs (Ill. 109), waves and (rarely) flowers in a rhomboid lattice (heart, Ill. 83, centre) or hook patterns (heart, Ill. 83, left). The ornamentation may be so imprecise that one cannot make out whether the silver background or the gilded elements are supposed to form the ornaments. Without being able to prove it, the author looks on pieces of this type, depending on their overall impression (traces of wear, delicacy of manufacture, quality of material), as representing a late style that cannot have originated before the twenties or thirties of this century. The frequency of these pieces as opposed to those with clearer ornamentation supports this view. According to Janata, the lines of the drawing were 'drawn mostly with punches and much more rarely with gravers.' In our material, traces of both techniques can be established by direct comparison. On the subject of fire gilding he says: 'The craftsman has covered the pattern ground with a resist paste (similar to

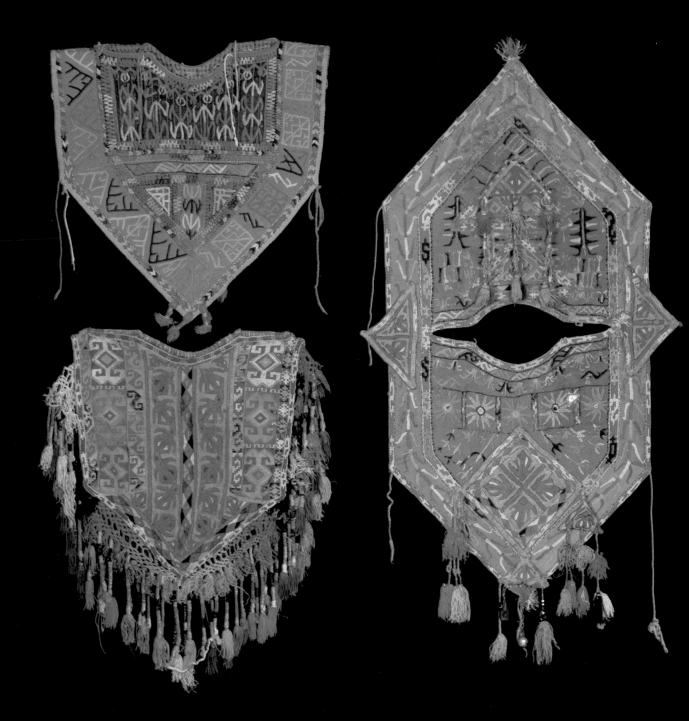

*Ill.'85b   Children's bibs from northern Afghanistan. The upper piece and
the right-hand piece clearly show the embroidery style of north
Afghan Turkmen. In the lower piece the embroidery styles of the
Turkmen (inside) and Lakai Uzbek (outside) were used side by side*

*Ill. 86   Embroidered trouser turnups of north Afghan Turkmen. The pieces
below right form part of male costume and are tucked into buzkashi
boots. All the other items were at the end of women's trouserlegs.
As the embroideries were a good deal stronger than the thin cotton
trousers, they were cut off and re-used when the trousers wore out*

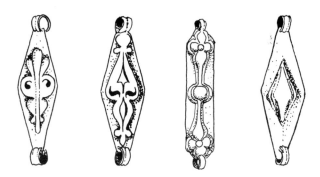

Ill. 87 Different north Afghan Turkmen armlets with engraved, stamped and appliqué decor, all of them silver without fire gilding. Above right, with cornelians. The pair illustrated below left come from Ersari from the Aqcha region; I have been unable to classify the other items. D.: from 6.3 to 6.7 cm; H. from 4.2 to 9.6 cm

Ill. 88 Connecting links of Turkmen jewellery. (Embossed in matrices.)

the batik technique in the field of textiles) and then followed the fire gilding in which process the gold only adhered in the places which were not covered.' This gilding technique seems to be used in pieces with very thick gilding and ornamentation which is much blurred. In pieces with more sparing ornamentation standing out clearly on the silver ground (Ill. 92), it is more likely, in our opinion, that the amalgam (v. Technology of metal working) was transferred to the silver ground with a brush. Fire gilded pieces in which the gilding seems unusually thick, slightly arched in section (i. e. the surface tension of the material is still recognisable) and clumsy form a special group. Microscopic examination of most fire gilded pieces shows signs that the gilding was polished with an agate. These signs are missing in the last-named group. It may be a peculiarity of the jewellery of a specific sub-tribe or workshop (Ill. 138).

Ersari jewellery is characterised by the absence of fire gilding and 'elegance and lightness in line drawing' (Ill. 81). Cornelians are used, but are not so predominant as in Teke jewellery. According to Janata, gilding is also absent among

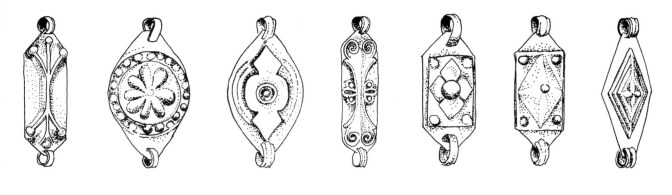

Ill. 89   Connecting links of Turkmen jewellery. (Embossed in matrices.)

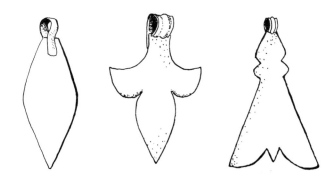

Ill. 90   Pendants to Turkmen jewellery cut out of silverplate, the right-hand one in adamlyk (homunculus) shape

the Aq Atabay-Yomut, whose pieces are supposed to be mainly characterised by open work, and among the Saryk to whom he ascribes, besides a preference for simple forms, the excessive use of gallery wire (v. technology). Following him, we should attribute Ill. 118, above, and the heart in Ill. 83 to the Saryk. Janata speaks of the Qara-dashly, whose name is supposed to be linked with 'the coarsest of Turkmen styles' (Ill. 84) as another group whose jewellery has no fire gilding. Fairly reliably, in my opinion, of all these groups whose style of jewellery is supposed to be characterised by the use of pure silver we can only localise the Ersari style, in which besides the 'elegance' we find lightness of treatment and the almost complete absence of the otherwise favourite gallery wire. We should describe as Ersari the chain diadem (Ill. 71), the temple jewellery (Ill. 81), possibly the disk-shaped ornamental plate (Ill. 112), the amulet (Ill. 121, bottom right) and the bracelets with runner decor (Ill. 87). I am sure that all the other bracelets in this illustration come from northern Afghan

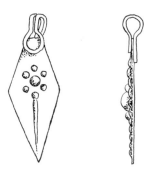

Ill. 91   Pendants embossed in flat matrices and enclosed on the rear side by soldering on sheet metal

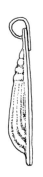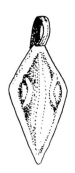

*Ill. 93   Pendants embossed in troughlike matrices and enclosed on the rear
side by soldering on sheet metal*

Turkmen. In the present state of knowledge, more precise attributions can only be the outcome of reading the tea leaves.

In contrast, the style of jewellery attributed to the Jafarbay Yomut is unmistakable. They are either completely covered with fire gilded silverplate (e. g. bracelet Ill. 119, bottom left) or have mostly rhomboid small silver plates soldered on to the base material. In every case, the decor of these appliqué elements is driven in precisely worked matrices and is unusually fine and dainty (Ill. 106, left). Older pieces are often set with *big* cornelians, sometimes together with glass beads in *muted* colours, whereas more recent pieces are characterised by the lack of big cornelians and the application of colourful, bright glass beads.

More varied than the ornamentation of the jewellery are the ways of shaping the edges of mostly Teke pieces and the pendants decorating many pieces of jewellery, chased in matrices or simply cut out of silverplate. In their forms, too, – in connection with the pieces on which they appear –

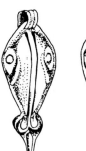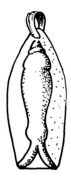

*Ill. 94   Variations of the pendants above: the two on the left shaped like
fish*

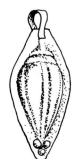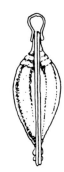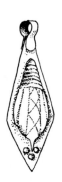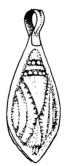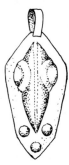

*Ill. 95   Pendants in the round. Two parts embossed in troughlike matrices
were soldered together*

*Ill. 92   Pectoral jewellery. Left: lozenge-shaped pendant, silver firegilded
with cornelians, mounted on silk, Teke, 19th c. Right: silver with
glass stones on cotton. Stamped décor (false granulation, cf. Ill. 130)
and engraved décor. Jewellery in the Kazak style, probably from
north Afghan Uzbeks. L.: 47 cm and 56 cm*

Ill. 97   Upper terminations of items of Teke jewellery. Stylised birds and flowers?

Ill. 98   Upper terminations of items of Teke jewellery in trefoil form

we can assume that there are indications of local workshops or specific tribal peculiarities. In drawings, we show – without claiming to be exhaustive – the wide range from our material. Pendants may be rhomboid, pointed oval, three-leaved or shaped like 'adamlyk', homunculi. They were chased in matrices which leave only the decor outstanding (Ill. 91). The pendant may be beaten in a trough-shaped matrix and closed on the rear side by straight sheet metal (Ill. 93) or two similar trough-shaped forms may be soldered together (Ill. 95). The simplest pendants have floral decor; then there are leaf and fruit shapes, forms suggesting beetles or larvae and fish forms, and even faces. Round bells are a standard form (Ill. 123), especially the pendants on amulets. The basic forms of the connecting links often combined with pendants are rhomboid, hexagonal or oval (Ill. 89). No regularity can be established for their decor. In the case of both pendants and connecting pieces, it is true that the basic form can be considerably varied by the different ways in which it is cut out. As a rule more complex forms occur in the more carefully worked pieces. Pendants in the round predominate in Teke material, flat pendants in Ersari pieces.

The commonest upper terminations or outer edges are rams' horns or forms that seen straight on remind us of rams' heads (Ill. 99). Other terminating shapes might be interpreted as bird representations or double-headed birds (eagles), as known since Seljuk times. Among vegetable motifs trefoils and flowers (tulips?) are recognisable. The formally still relatively clear terminations we have mentioned are usually cast or chased in matrices and soldered or, as in illustration 98, they consist of magnificent cleanly executed pierced work on pieces with otherwise clear ornaments. On pieces with flatter, vaguer ornamentation, the terminations often seem to be sawn out or pierced after patterns and only allow us to guess at the original models (Ill. 100).

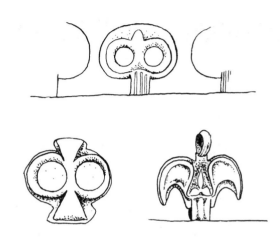

Ill. 99   Upper terminations of items of Turkmen jewellery. Stylised rams' heads or rams' horns?

Ill. 96   Turkestan dorsal pigtail jewellery, cotton with silk embroidery. Left: Ersari. Centre: the style of embroidery is reminiscent of decorative yurt bands, which are presumed to have originated before 1900, according to our informants; the silver appliqué could point to the Ersari. Right: The technique of embroidery and ornamentation reminiscent of susanis indicate a provenance in the environs of Bukhara. It might have been made for an Uzbek or Tadhzik woman, L.: from 46 to 59 cm

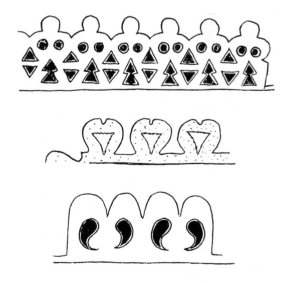

Ill. 100   Perforated or sawn out terminations which produce a highly standardised effect

Typology of Turkestan Jewellery

We shall now try to present the most important types of jewellery classified according to the part of the body on which they are worn. The Linden Museum Turkmen collection appears to be typologically complete. Although it is certainly the most comprehensive museum collection outside the eastern block, to the best of our knowledge, there are appreciable gaps when it comes to urban material. Types that are not represented will merely be mentioned. The indigenous words for the items of jewellery are given in the abovementioned works.

Head Jewellery

The various types of Turkmen frontal jewellery are often described en bloc as bridal crowns. This applies to the high frontlet (Ill. 103). Their counterpart in urban jewellery, which undoubtedly originated under Russian influence, is the bridal crown, Ill. 104, which is made up of many small parts, richly ornamented with semi-precious stones or, as from ca. 1900, glass stones. Examples of it in a similar form appear in most of the larger towns in Turkestan.

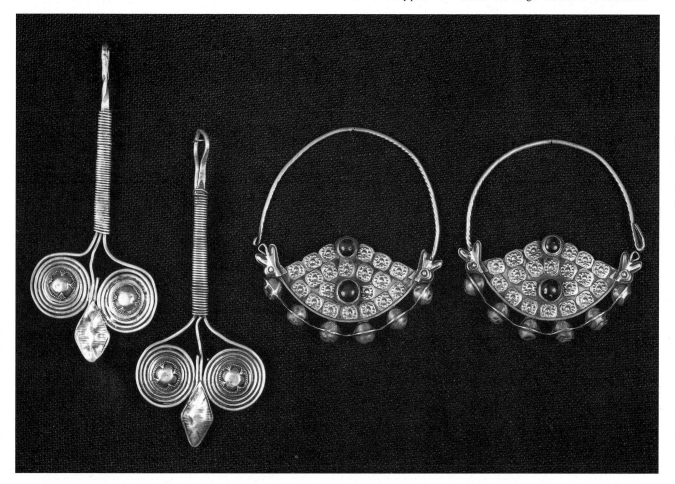

Ill. 101 Frontal jewellery: above: chain diadem, silver, fire gilded with cornelians, Teke Turkmen. Centre: silver pendants and pearls, red glass beads on cotton, Ersari. Below: Diadem with hanging chains, silver with glass beads, Qattaghan Uzbek, northern Afghanistan. W. 53.5 cm, 43 cm, 24 cm

Ill. 102 Two Iranian Turkmen pairs of earrings, silver; the right-hand pair with fire gilded appliqué and glass stones. Length of left-hand pair, 12 cm, d. of right-hand pair, 8.5 cm

*Ill. 103   Ornamental frontal plate which forms part of bridal jewellery.
Silver, fire gilded with cornelians and glass stones, Teke Turkmen,
late 19th/early 20th c. 18.5 cm by 27.5 cm*

Chain and articulated diadems (Ill. 71 and 101) are generally part of the jewellery of married women. However, girls' caps with small articulated diadems sewn on to them are also known. From Khiva we know gilded articulated diadems set with turquoises and coral, the upper edges of which form double-headed birds. (Ill. 114 and 164). From the Uzbeks of Qattaghan, northern Afghanistan, we know pure silver articulated diadems with a round disk in the centre and two rectangular shapes to right and left, chased decoration reminiscent of granulation and glass bead additions. All the diadems mentioned were sewn on to the head adornment. From the Ersari we know diadems which consist of articulated hairpins terminating in powerful rams' heads and which, as A. Stucki's illustrations show, were worn in combination with Teke articulated dia-

dems. Among the Ersari (Ill. 101 centre), separate red and silver glass or plastic beads sewn on to a fabric backing form a border with geometric patterns. Round decorative disks connected by chains were sewn on to women's high caps as were the crescent-shaped decorative plates, sometimes published as pectoral jewellery (e. g. Prokot) whose engraved decoration corresponds to the style of the bracelet on the left of Ill. 87. (In the Linden Museum collection there is a women's cap from northern Afghanistan which has a crescent-shaped plate sewn on to the brow side. But judging by a drawing by Wasiljewa the disks normally seem to be attached to the bonnet in such as way that they can only be seen from above).

A shape of frontal jewellery, described by Janata as an 'almond moon', consists of three boteh patterns aranged in a half-moon. It should undoubtedly be classified with the rich, colourful filigree-like Khiva jewellery, with its excessive use of coral and turqoise. During recent years pieces of this kind have come on to the market in large numbers.

Ill. 104 *Bridal crown which was part of the jewellery of an Uzbek or Tadzhik bride in Samarkand, silver, fire gilded with ornamental stones and glass, late 19th c. 14 by 24 cm*

Their purpose is not clear. The author has frequently been told that they are turban jewellery, which seems possible in comparison with contemporary Iranian and Indian turban jewellery, but we cannot exclude their use as female jewellery. From the Lakai we know embroidered frontlets with gilded bottle-shaped elements sewn on to them (rose-water flasks? Ill. 71 and 105).

Ill. 105 *Gilded silver element, set with turquoises and glass beads, in the form of a rose-water flask, which was sewn on to an embroidered frontlet of the Lakai Uzbek*

Ill. 106   Pigtail jewellery. Left: Yomut, silver with firegilded appliqué; the three cornelians on the bar in the middle are so mounted that they are transparent. Right: Item of urban jewellery from Khiva. silver, filigree, fire gilded, set with turquoises, glass stones and coral. Culmination in the form of a double-headed bird twice repeated. The key pendants have significance as amulets. From left to right: 45.5 cm, 39 cm

Ill. 107   Combination piece from Khiva, silver, fire gilded, turquoises and glass stones, consisting of earrings, pectoral ornament with amulet holders and pigtail jewellery. H.: c. 42 cm

Hair and Dorsal Jewellery, Plait Jewellery, Temple and Ear Jewellery

This group is even more varied than frontal jewellery. Apart from small pendants, which may well form part of everyday dress, there is a broad spectrum of more complicated pieces of jewellery composed of many separate elements which can only be items of festive dress because they would be too cumbersome for the daily round. Firouz, too, mentions only a few silver coins or elements which are still in everyday use.

Pendants made up of several elements and up to 60 cm long worn on the temples occur among the Ersari (Ill. 81) and the Yomut (Ill. 106, left, one of a pair with cornelians mounted so as to be transparent). The parts of these pendants (among the Ersari) or at least the uppermost part (among the Yomut) are depicted as adamlyk = homunculi. So they are probably human figures which have significance as amulets. Both Yomut and Ersari temple pendants may be closely connected with chain diadems. Urban counterparts can be found in Khiva jewellery. Gilded turqoise-studded silver components are combined with coral and black silk tassels into two or three-row pendants, which terminate in a knot reminiscent of the Buddhist knot of happiness. A most unusual type for our understanding of jewellery is a combination piece in typical Khiva style consisting of earrings with temple pendants leading from them, as well as a tripartite pectoral ornament (Ill. 107).

The most striking example of dorsal jewellery hanging from the back of the head or the two pigtails is found among the Teke. Large heart- or double-heart-shaped plates (Ills. 83, 108), or very small hearts worn in a row of three

(Ill. 108) form the centre of this item of jewellery. They are frequently combined with articulated (Ill. 109, left) and coin chains, into which small triangular cloth amulets are often incorporated. The Teke appendages of spherical and chased dome-shaped pendants, rarely found on the market, reach considerable dimensions and weight. The dorsal appendages of the Jafarbay Yomut are generally even more articulated and terminate in three dome-shaped pendants or small hearts (Ill. 109, right). Ill. 106 shows a magnificent example of an urban dorsal appendage from Khiva with gilding, filigree, elements chased in matrices, turquoises and large corals. A twice-repeated double-headed bird forms the upper edge; the key pendants below surely have significance as amulets (the key to paradise?). From rural Uzbeks and Turkmen we know dorsal ornaments of black woven cotton strips with colourful stitched seams in the middle and flat round sewn on small silver plates whose floral decoration is beaten in matrices.

Ill. 96 shows a type of pigtail or dorsal ornament which is still unpublished to the best of our knowledge. It consists of embroidered bands which may also form bags. From

Ill. 108 Heart- and double-heart-shaped Teke dorsal jewellery, silver, fire gilded with cornelians; pieces like the small heart, far right, were worn in threes. H.: from 13.5 to 17.5 cm

Ill. 109 Turkmen dorsal appendages. Right: Yomut, silver, cornelians, fire gilded appliqué. Left: Teke, silver, fire gilded, cornelians, hung with Iranian silver coins and triangular cotton amulet holder. From left to right: 59.5 cm and 59 cm

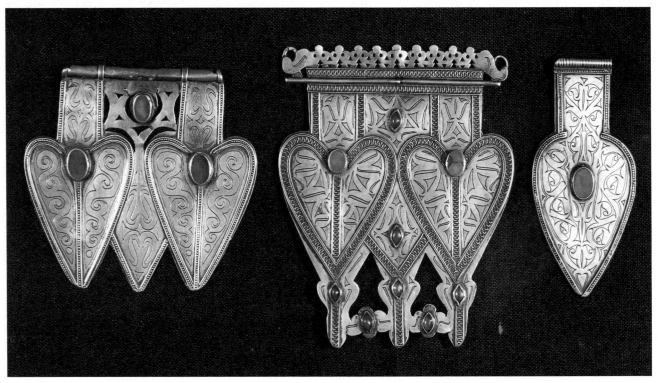

their style of embroidery, two of the items obviously come from the Turkmen of northern Afghanistan, one in the typical susani style of embroidery must have an urban provenance.

In the Teke style we know triangular pieces extended below rectangularly or pear-shaped pieces which can be hung directly from the ear by a curved spike or worn on a leather band over the head and then dangled over the ears. Basket-shaped earrings with dragon heads on both sides and pure silver heart-shaped earrings occur among the Iranian Turkmen. The basket-shaped items exhibit obvious features of the Yomut style (Ill. 102).

Ill. 117 exhibits a selection of urban ear and false ear jewellery. The pure silver appendages incorporating coloured glass beads, upper left, are typical examples of Tadzhik jewellery from the beginning of the 20th century; the right-hand earrings with their rather insistent splendour come from Khiva. Earrings composed of three spheroids, like ours from the Ferghana valley, have been shown to go back to the jewellery of ancient South Arabia and pre-

Ill. 110   *Turkmen necklace. Left: Yomut, silver, fire gilded appliqué, cornelians, D. 17 cm, h. 14.5 cm. Right: Teke, silver, fire gilded, cornelians. Horseshoe-shaped necklace with hooks, which terminate in animal heads and much articulated ornamental plate with fish-shaped appendages as its lower termination. D. 18 cm, h. 26.5 cm*

Ill. 111   *Necklace, silver, fire gilded with cornelians, of three linked elements, Teke. The necklaces were supposed to be worn with large hexagonal hanging pectoral plates. The item illustrated does not belong to the necklet. W. of band: 14 cm, w. of plate: 33 cm*

Islamic Iran and had spread throughout the Islamic world even in the age of the first Caliphs. The rectangular pure gold false ear pendants set with numerous ornamental stones form an exception in our collection; they were certainly owned by royalty (Bukhara). The heavy silver turquoise studded small earrings next to them probably also come from Bukhara.

Neck and Pectoral Jewellery

Here, too, the most powerful and impressive ornaments stem from the Teke. Unornamented horseshoe-shaped necklets terminate in hooks which may end in animal heads. From these hooks hangs a highly articulated pierced ornamental plate (Ill. 110). In the Yomut variation of this type, which strikes one as much more delicate and dainty – obviously an influence of the refined urban culture of Iran – one side of the ornamental plate is riveted to the necklet, the other closes by a pin fixed to a chain. Our piece is primarily characterised by the unusual austerity in the décor of the ornamental plate. (The pieces are said to have also been worn as frontal jewellery. A detailed discussion of the problem is found in Prokot and in Rudolph.) Because of their articulation, the above-mentioned Teke pectorals create a relatively light effect. On the other hand, necklets with straight rectangular frontal closures, mostly divided into three elements with a large rhomboid decorative plate hanging from them, look more like armour than jewellery (Ill. 111; plate and band do not belong to each other, but the method of wearing has been abundantly proven). A special type of necklet found only among the Yomut can be seen in Ill. 84 on the left. A massive silver band was twisted and an oval plate decorated in the Yomut style was attached to it by hooks and eyes. The piece on the right of Ill. 84 is attributed to an Iranian Turkmen group; it also shows elements of Yomut décor.

The collar-studs mainly known from the Yomut, but also from the Teke, can fairly be described as functional neck ornaments. Among all the mentioned Turkmen groups, round and rhomboid pendants, individually or in pairs, were worn as pectoral ornaments. They could be sewn directly on to the clothing or worn over a cloth foundation like a bib (Ill. 92, Ill. 118). (Prokot's interpretation of the round disk as a solar symbol and amulet cannot be dismissed out of hand, but nor can it be proved, to the best of my knowledge). A similar solution is shown to the right of Ill. 92. Three foils connected by chains are mounted on cloth and worn as a collar or cravat. The piece shown was bought in northern Afghanistan and is probably of Kazak origin. Similar jewellery, as Janata has conclusively shown, must have been made for the Uzbeks in the Kazak style in northern Afghanistan. In the present state of research, it cannot be affirmed whether this is a case of

Ill. 112 Disk-shaped pectoral jewellery; north Afghan Turkmen? The décor is chased, appliqué and stamped. The second piece from above comes from the environs of Aqcha. The ornamentation makes it reasonable to classify it as Ersari jewellery. But the use of blue and red glass beads makes a rural Uzbek group a more likely choice. D. from 5.3 to 10.3 cm

recent influences of the Kazak style or whether the close proximity of both groups led to joint enterprises in earlier times. Turkestan's non-Tadzhik urban neck ornamentation is closer to the Russian than the Islamic tradition of jewellery. Pectorals with long articulated chains and trapezoid plates which are fire gilded all over and set with bright glass beads represent the late style of Yomut jewellery and probably did not originate before the 40s or 50s of this century (Ill. 82, centre). Combined netlike pectoral ornaments of glass beads and silver disks chased in matrices are attributed to Uzbeks in rural northern Afghanistan, so far without proof.

At present, the wide variety of most ornaments sewn on to clothing cannot be covered completely. Ill. 116, right, shows a standard shape. The piece on the left of the same plate is reminiscent of carpet or felt décor and is unique, as far as I know. In the centre is an amulet which is normally sewn on and which reminds Janata of a 'baroque-style' two-headed eagle. Scholars have also seen in it a lingering of the Seljuk tradition. A piece from a private collection (Ill. 23) shows a marked similarity to the Tsarist two-headed eagle. It was well-known throughout Turkestan from coins and from the trademark on Gardener porcelain, whereas the Seljuk double eagle as opposed to the two-headed eagle cannot be proved after the 14th century. Until there is evidence to the contrary, we shall assume the adoption of Russian models. Shapes like pots (Ill. 183) and feet, cut out of silverplate, occur as small coat pendants. Our horse-shaped pendant (Ill. 17) is a unique piece which provides impressive proof of the achievements metal workers were capable of in a completely alien métier. We only know the representation of horses – in this case with a rider – in one further example, as the image inside a heart-shaped plate (Ill. 186). Even for such a horseloving people as the Turkmen, the fear of depicting living creatures ordained by religion seems to have persisted.

Ill. 113 Disk-shaped pectoral jewellery. Above: Teke, the two lower items from Iranian groups, the central one possibly Goklan (after Firouz). D. from 10 to 12 cm

Previous two pages

Ill. 114   Khiva head jewellery. Diadem, pigtail ornaments and veil, silver, partially fire gilded, turquoises and coral, cotton. W. of diadem: 42 cm, l. of pigtail ornaments: 30/38 cm l. of veil: 57 cm

Ill. 115   Works by Bukharan silversmiths. Nielloing and enamelling are the typical Bukhara decorative techniques. The two round disks are belt fittings. The left-hand one is silver, with émail champlevé partially fire gilded, the right-hand one, nielloed silver. Above right: two-part belt fastener, nielloed silver. Between the coarse runners on the oval central part, the remains of wax inlay. Centre: rouge holder, silver, enamelled, appendage with coral and baroque pearls; on the inserted rouge stick, a sitting bird. Below left: Upper arm amulet for men, rear side silver with émail cloisonné. The front side consists of a bloodstone with the carved text of a Shiite prayer. W. from 8 to 14 cm

Ill. 116   Pieces of jewellery in the Teke style which are sewn on to the clothing. The centre item, a highly stylised double-headed eagle has significance as an amulet. But we may also assume that the other two pieces had value as amulets. The shape of the left-hand piece is extremely rare. H. from 8.3 to 25 cm

Ill. 117   Ear and temple jewellery from Turkestan towns. Above left: temple jewellery, silver with glass stones and coral, Samarkand, early 20th c. Next to it: earrings, silver, fire gilded, coral, turquoises, glass, Khiva, end of 19th c. Below, from left to right: earrings, silver, fire gilded, Ferghana, temple jewellery, gold with baroque pearls and ornamental stones; the pieces are supposed to come from Bukhara and may have been owned by princes. Earrings, silver with turquoises, Bukhara? All end of 19th/beginning of 20th c. L. from 6.5 to 17.5 cm

124

Arm, Hand and Finger jewellery

The multiplicity of sleeve-like Turkmen bracelets has already been mentioned when describing the various ornamental styles. Teke bracelets may be considered the 'classical type'. They are usually segmented (Ill. 119). (Prokot and Rudolph give impressive surveys.) According to our observations, bracelets with three or four segments are the standard format. There are pairs which have as many as six or even eight segments (Ill. in Rudolph; Prokot points to a pair with eight segments in the Historical Museum of Ashkhabad.) The different shapes of the claws forming the internal fastening probably indicate the style of workshops or localities. The use of flat or dome-shaped cornelians may depend not only on availability, but also on the specifications of a particular workplace. There are no urban bracelets in our collection. We do know narrow open silver bracelets with partial gilding and niello décor. (Tschjyri also names copper, silver and brass bracelets, open or closed, with stamped and/or engraved décor, as well as filigree bracelets and items of pearl and coral.) The whole group seems hard

Ill. 118 Rhomboid pectoral jewellery worn individually or in pairs. Above: north Afghanistan, presumably Saryk. Below: standard Teke piece. Right: unusually delicate Teke work. H. from 28 to 30.5 cm

Ill. 119 Turkestan armlets. Above left: pair of armlets in the 'Kazak style', silver and cloth based glass stones. Right: Silver, fire gilded, cornelians and appliqué small silver plates. The piece was acquired in Kabul and must have come from a north Afghan group we have not been able to identify. Below left: Yomut armbands. Right: Teke bracelets with four segments. D. from 6.3 to 7.2 cm, h. from 6 to 11.5 cm

Ill. 120 Finger rings. The three rings on the far left of silver with cornelians or an engraved ornamental plate are of north Afghan Turkmen origin, the four adjoining rings exhibit fire gilding and can be attributed to the Teke. The four rings in the right-hand half of the picture with false granulation and colourful glass backing can be classified in the Kazak style, but may come from a north Afghan Uzbek group. Length of ornamental plates: from 2 to 6.5 cm

to encompass compared with Turkmen bracelets or even with other types of urban jewellery. We can but await enlightenment when Soviet collections are published. Ill. 119, upper left, shows a pair of Kazak or Uzbek bracelets. The décor is characterised by a sparing use of fire gilding, colourful glass beads, an exceptionally fine stamped floral pattern and false 'granulation', also stamped. Careful examination of traces of wear indicate that the pieces are genuinely old. Janata has mentioned that the quest for pieces of this kind in Afghanistan has resulted in a flood of copies. The copies are so good that the authenticity of genuine pieces is often questioned.

'Hand roses', which consist of a narrow bracelet, a plate ornamenting the back of the hand and finger-rings connected by chains are a peculiarity of Turkmen jewellery. All the pieces known to us have extremely clumsy workmanship in common. These hand roses have their prototype in the ornamental tradition of the Indian subcontinent. Finger-rings are usually the last items of jewellery with which the owner parts, so they are rarely represented in collections and published. Ill. 120 shows three Turkmen rings from northern Afghanistan on the left, next to four Teke rings. In the right half of the picture we can see four Kazak or Uzbek rings 'in the Kazak style'. The largest of these rings has two finger-rings behind the ornamental plate. According to Janata, this necessarily makes it the property of a female Kazak matchmaker. The depiction of two toads in the ring would fit in with this interpretation, as they are widely known as fertility symbols – a décor that would tally with the owner's occupation. The urban rings illustrated by Tschjyri apparently do not differ essentially from contemporary European or – occasionally – Iranian examples.

Ill. 121 *Written amulet holders. Above left: silver, fire gilded, turquoises, coral and glass stone, filigree décor, Khiva, 19th c. Right: silver, fire gilded, cornelians, Teke, end of 19th/ beginning of 20th c. Below left: silver, colourful glass backing, sparse fire gilding, Kazak or Uzbek in Kazak style. Right: silver with cornelians, Ersari. W. from 9.5 to 23 cm*

Ill. 122 *'Hand rose', silver, cornelians, glass stones, Ersari. Bracelets with hanging jewellery for the back of the hand and finger rings are characteristic of north Afghan Turkmen jewellery and may have originated under Indian influence. D. of bracelet; 5.8 cm, l.: 22 cm*

Amulets

Turkmen amulets in particular have unmistakably independent shapes, but we must remember that amulets are a vital part of popular belief in the Islamic world, although official Islamic theology refuted them altogether. But belief in the efficaciousness of amulets against disease, evil spirits and the evil eye cannot be expelled from the people's minds. Among the superficially islamised steppe dwellers, amulets obviously play a greater role than in Turkestan towns which were strongholds of Islamic spirituality in the Middle Ages and whose inhabitants were much more under the control of conservative Islamic priestly thinking. Nevertheless, members of the same priesthood were responsible for producing the written amulets, which were then placed in the widest variety of amulet holders. The texts included passages from the Koran, incantations from magical books handed down from the early Middle Ages, enumeration of the putative 99 'Beautiful names of God', supplications to angels and saints, or magic squares whose total gave the name of God, an angel or a reference to a Sura in the Koran*). But this aspect of amulets which is

---

*) A. Janata, 1981, has published a brief, but most instructive account of amulets in Afghanistan, which is recommended as an introduction to the subject.

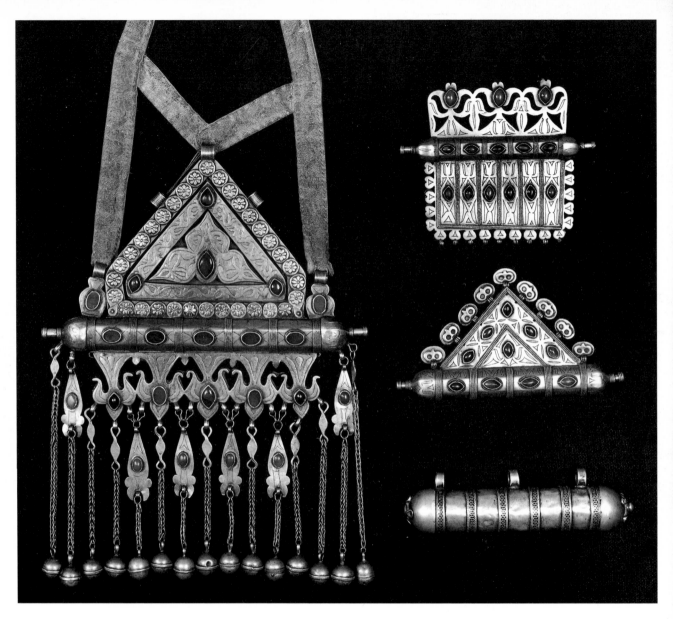

still not eradicated from Islamic religious thinking relates not only to the upper and most obvious conceptual layer. An underlying stratum has its roots in ancient oriental traditions and similar ones which originated in the Mediterranean in prehistoric times. Even the materials used to make amulets had a significance. Pure white silver was associated with the moon. Moon goddesses played an important part in religion in Pre-islamic Arabia and distant parts of the Ancient East. Red cornelian, the 'bloodstone', was supposed to protect from bleeding, wounds and miscarriages, blue turquoise against the evil eye, which was always con-

Ill. 123 Amulet holders. The most important element of this piece of jewellery which has value as an amulet is a cylindrical or prism-shaped holder which can always be opened in the case of large pieces. It is intended to house written amulets. Among north Afghan Turkmen, the holder can be reduced to this basic form (below right). The other three pieces come from the Teke. Small holders were sewn on to the clothing in pairs; large ones, such as the left-hand one, were part of bridal jewellery and worn only on festive occasions. W. from 15.5 to 25.5 cm, h. from 10 to 35 cm

Ill. 124 Flank ornamentation for bridal camels. Above: silk embroidery on cotton ground, Teke. Below: knotted work, Yomut. The pieces were worn in pairs; embroidered examples are very rare. 73 by 150 cm and 96 by 118 cm

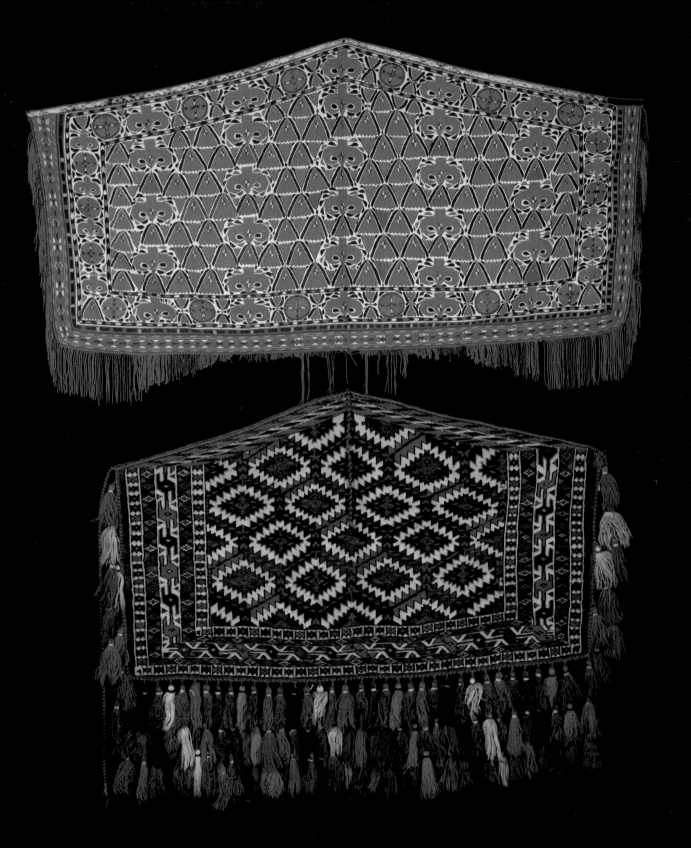

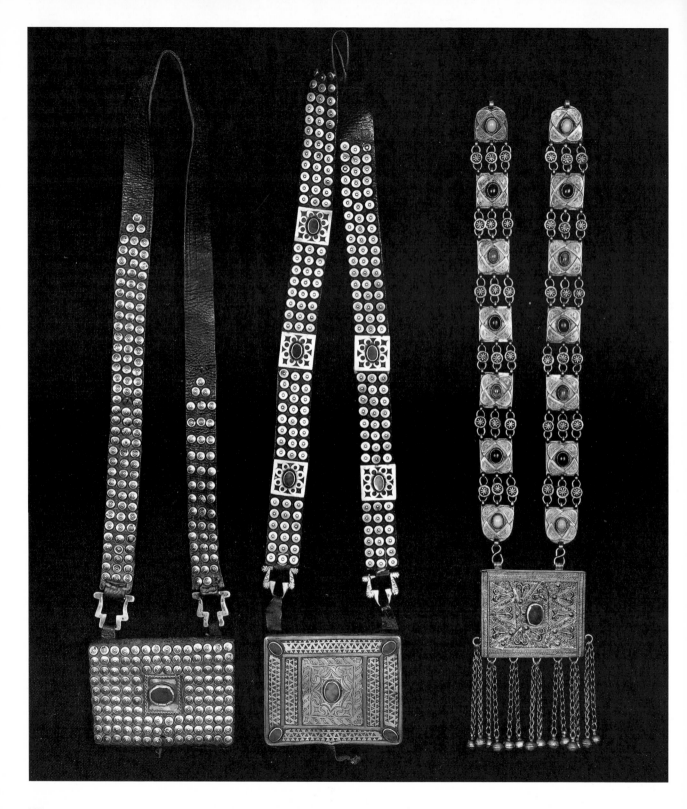

Ill. 125 Older Turkmen women's amulet pouches. Left: Ersari, centre: Teke, both leather with silver fittings and cornelians; the Teke piece has fire gilding. Right: Yomut, silver, set with fire gilded appliqué, cornelians and glass stones. H. from 56.5 to 62.5 cm, w. from 9 to 13 cm

Ill. 126 Amulets from Turkestan towns. Above: bow-shaped amulets, the left-hand one combined with triangular amulet holders, silver, fire gilded with cornelians and turquoises, Khiva, 19th c. Below: Amulet holder from Samarkand, silver partially fire gilded with niello décor and glass stones, Samarkand, beginning of 20th c. H. from 15.5 to 22.5 cm, w. from 10.5 to 12 cm

Ill. 127   Turkmen bridal procession. The bride sits in an enclosed litter to the right of the centre of the picture, before 1890

nected with blue eyes in places where they are rare. (Danger always comes from outsiders; the witch with the humpback.) The colour, not the material, is the most effective agent. So cornelian can be replaced by coral (in urban jewellery) and turquoise by glass stones. The shape of the amulet also has its own significance. The most frequently found triangle (Ill. 121), an ancient universal symbol of female fertility, is still a powerful means of averting danger. (Because it could not be eradicated from popular belief, the eye of God inside a triangle was later introduced into Christian art.) One symbol of male fertility, the phallus, is the fish, which we find as a pendant to items of Turkmen jewellery. Equally old and universal symbols of strength are animal claws and teeth, which symbolise courage, power and agility. Small wonder then that they appear as amulets for boys, together with bowshaped amulets, obviously intended to protect from wounds and attacks. There is evidence of birds and double-headed birds (eagles) as an emblem of sovereignty (cf. Janata) in the Near East as early as the third millennium. They also play an important part in the jewellery and amulet tradition of the peoples of Turkestan. But birds also have a part in shamanistic ideology as a link between the various levels and they can symbolise the sun. The commonly found crosswise division of rhomboid pendants could also be a survival of shamanistic thinking, with the crosspiece representing the four points of the compass and the emphasised centre the world's axis. Nor would

I exclude the possibility that the figure five has a symbolic meaning, although Janata doubts this. It is almost compulsory in the ornamentation of rhomboid plates. But when five cornelians occur so often on hearts (Ill. 83), decorate the centre of frontal plates (Ill. 103), and the hexagonal or octagonal prism-shaped elements of amulet holders holding the writing are often segmented fivefold and studded with five cornelians, we find it a trail worth further investigation. The view of D. Gulsoltan mentioned by J. Prokot that the heart-shaped dorsal ornamental plates signalised the desire for fertility and children and are a symbol of love seems to me to rely too heavily on European popular beliefs to be conclusive. The men who first interpreted the symbols correctly have undoubtedly been dead for thousands of years. A great deal may also have been the esoteric knowledge of a small group of religious officials, magicians and witches. The shapes and symbols themselves have survived in jewellery and amulets. The frequently expressed view that women's desire for amulets was alone responsible for the early development of jewellery is surely untenable in that blunt form. After all, men, too, are exposed to danger and have to protect themselves, heal diseases, etc. Men, too, wear amulets, mostly written amulets which are simply sewn into a piece of cloth. Side by side with the desire to wear amulets, aesthetic and economic needs played at least an equal role in the initial stages of jewellery. In other words, until proof to the contrary, we are entitled to but not forced to think that every item of jewellery has significance as an amulet. The discussion about amulets and jewellery, moreover, will make no sense to a Muslim, because the separation of the religious and profane spheres, which even with

us is only a product of modern times, is incomprehensible to him.

No sphere of the mental culture of non-European peoples is so lightly mocked as that of magic. In my opinion, we should be sparing with our mockery. Throughout the world man faces dangers and problems that cannot be mastered by rational means. Attempts to solve them are not too far apart. In our opinion, there is no real difference between the practising Catholic who keeps a medallion of St Christopher in his car and the Turkmen who hangs a triangular cloth with a written amulet sewn into it from his horse's bridle, between the Catholic woman who wears a medallion of the Virgin Mary round her neck and the Turkmen woman who wears an amulet holder. Both are trying to ensure the protection of supernatural powers from dangers they see no defence against.

Ill. 121 shows at one glance the most important type of written amulet holder with a round or prism-shaped capsule in the styles of the Ersari and Teke, to the right, and of Kazak and urban jewellery from Khiva to the left. Smaller holders of this type were sewn on in pairs, larger ones (as in Ill. 123, left) were worn individually on a ribbon or a chain. Only the large holders are made to open. The smaller ones are soldered up. Whether they ever held writing or whether the form stands for the content, which is quite conceivable, must remain an open question. Sometimes the triangular holders lack the usual pendants. Rectangular shapes are rare. Reduction to a cylindrical holder which serves only to receive the writing is common in Ersari jewellery (Ill. 123). The written amulets described so far are worn by young women. In their place, older women wear individual silvermounted leather pouches, diagonally or crosswise in pairs, which already struck earlier travellers because of their similarity to cartridge-pouches. Similar holders made of metal and opening at the side are the commonest amulet holders among the Yomut; simpler, smaller, rectangular holders were sewn onto the clothing. Ill. 126, below, shows a nielloed amulet holder, set with blue glass beads, which formed part of the trousseau of a Samarkand bride. Above, the two bows and the combined bow and triangular amulet in typical Khiva style may have originated under Turkmen influence. We know nothing about how they were worn.

An upper arm amulet for men comes from Bukhara (Ill. 115, below left). The enamelled reverse side shows marked indications of Moghul enamelled work. The front carries a bloodstone, with an engraved inscription showing that its wearer must have been a Shiite. It is divided into four fields. The outermost one contains Sura 2/54 of the Koran, followed by a prayer to Ali to intercede with Muhammed. The next field contains appeals to Muhammed, Fatima (the prophet's daughter) and the twelve Imams. The concluding prayer in the centre says: 'We seek protection through God's magnificence and greatness and also through God's messenger Muhammed'.

The Dating of Turkmen Jewellery

The question of the age of Turkmen jewellery has long been the subject of animated discussions in collecting and academic circles, but they have not enabled us to make more than estimations, apart from the rare dated items. The oldest dated piece in the Linden Museum collection is the horse's head-gear (Ill. 5); it bears the date 1264 Hegira, i. e. 1847 AD. The author himself has seen dated hearts, bracelets and amulets in the shape of double-headed eagles. All the dates lie between 1321 and 1337 Hegira (1903 and 1918 AD).

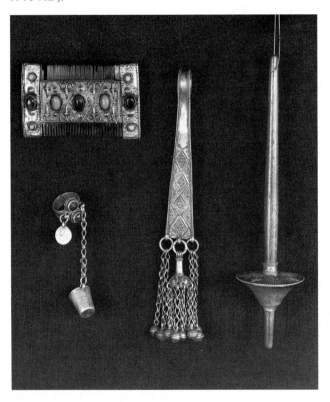

Ill. 128   Personal effects of Yomut women. Horn comb with gilded silver fittings and glass stones. Ring with thimble, weight for holding down the end of the thread and spindle (wooden rod restored) silver with gilded appliqué. W. of comb: 9 cm; length of weight: 20.5 cm

Differences in style and the quality of workmanship between the oldest and most recently dated pieces are not such that we can establish even a relative chronology, given the very small number of such items. The date adopted by us for the cessation of Teke jewellery production at least must be appreciably later. That does not tally with Janata's assumption that 'the production of Turkmen jewellery (which should really be called Teke jewellery) obviously ceased around 1920'. On the other hand, after a stay among the Turkmen of Mangyshlak in 1909, Karutz wrote: 'I very seldom. . . saw a bracelet among the jewellery, and never the precious neck or frontal plates, or the bandoliers of Merv. However, many chests may still contain inherited pieces, which are only worn on special occasions; some were produced at my request, but they were all modern work.'

The material in chests considerably complicates any attempts at estimating dates. Items of jewellery in daily use, especially bracelets and small amulets often exhibit marked signs of wear and tear. Fire gilding may be reduced to remnants. Ornamental stones are broken off, the inner cover plate of bracelets is worn through at the edges, etc. Everything indicates that the items are quite old, but it would surprise us if a piece of this type coming on the market today were more than two or three generations old. Pieces of jewellery for the wedding dress or trousseau of a wealthy Turkmen woman (diadem, large amulet, 20 cm wide, five or six-tiered bracelets) may be dated to the beginning of the last century provided they survived the ups and downs of nomadic economy in the chest of a wealthy family.

Bridal jewellery has frequently been referred to in this chapter. The bride in all her glory was taken to the bridegroom's aul in ceremonial procession (Ill. 127). She sat on a camel in an enclosed litter (centre of picture). The decoration of this bridal camel must also be accounted part of the bridal décor in the widest sense. Mostly among the Yomut, we know embroidered covers with patchwork decor which extend from the camel's head over the litter and cover its back completely. Rectangular trappings using the same technique decorate the flanks (cf. Ill. 34). Better known as décor for the flanks of bridal camels are osmulduks, pentagonal or – more rarely – heptagonal pouch-like knotted products; they are always made in pairs. Embroidered camel ornamentation of the same form is one of the rare and most magnificent items of Turkmen textile art (Ill. 124).

It has become the practice to discuss personal effects ornamented in the jewellery technique together with jewellery. Objects of this kind used by women are mostly found in Yomut material (Ill. 128).

The Technology of Metal Decoration

Craftsmen

All the details in this chapter result from the examination of finished items of jewellery. Russian literature may contain the occasional systematic account of workshop techniques. We have none such available. Even the ethnic classification of craftsmen is difficult. The unanimous opinion is that the majority of urban craftsmen were Tadzhik. We have already mentioned that urban metal vessels were produced in collaboration. We can at least assume such worksharing for the urban silversmiths. Janata (1981) also believes in this division of work for the producers of Turkmen jewellery. 'It is highly probable that chasing, stamping and engraving on the one hand and gilding on the other were carried out by different specialists, of whom neither the one nor the other was necessarily the expert who first shaped the piece with its appliqué work, settings and pendants.' Given detailed investigation of items of jewellery often of the highest craftsmen's standard, Janata's assumption must persist. Once a certain standard of quality is reached, we think that only the towns can be considered as production centres of Turkmen jewellery. They must have been Merv and Khiva for the region of presentday Turkmenia, while Gorgan and Gonbad-e-Qabus come most readily to mind for Iran. A similar centre of production for northern Afghanistan cannot be established. The simpler less demanding jewellery may all have been produced by parttime rural silversmiths. We have however no information about such craftsmen in this field. There are details concerning agricultural Turkmen in König (*Achal Teke*). That would be a contribution to explaining the striking falling off in quality to be found among apparently contemporary Teke pieces. Wasiljewa mentions Murghab Turkmen, presumably Saryq. We have found no reliable proof of the existence of nomadic craftsmen.

Materials

The abundant metal resources in Turkestan were no longer exploited in the 19th century. Iranian, Russian and Chinese coins were smelted down as the basic material for most items of Turkestan jewellery. Consequently, the majority of such pieces have a silver content of between 800 and 900. Gold was obtained from Russian gold coins. Cornelian and coral were probably imported from India and Europe. The baroque pearls often found in urban pieces were also European imports. Turquoise used in urban districts could have come from Khorassan camp sites. Both European and locally produced glass beads seem to have been used.

Decorative Techniques*)

1) Engraving and stamping: Ill. 129

Engraving is a technique involving the removal of fragments of metal. Gravers are used to remove the material. In stamping, punches, i. e. 'chisel-like steel tools with smooth and patterned surfaces' (Janata) are placed on the piece and struck with a hammer in order to form patterns. Ill. 129 shows a detail of a bracelet, the contours of the tendril being engraved, the background being given a matt finish with a hollow punch.

---

*) *This summary is based on publications by Hirschberg and Janata, Janata 1981, and my own preliminary studies, 1976.*

2) Granulation and false granulation: Ill. 130

'Scraps of sheet metal or small pieces of wire heated in powdered charcoal run into globules, the bottoms of which are enriched with carbon monoxide. The base metal. . . is also heated and smeared with isinglass or a similar substance. The transferred globules fuse with it.' (Janata.) A superficially similar impression can be obtained by working a piece closely with a *perloir* (false granulation). Mistakes are impossible, because authentic granulation always remains on the surface of the piece of jewellery. Indentations in the surface can easily be seen in this detail of an Uzbek bridal crown.

3) Repoussé and chasing: Ill. 131

The sheet metal is carved by hammer blows. The piece is either laid on a concave surface and worked from inside or placed on a convex surface and worked from outside. When a relief is formed in the sheet metal from the back with a modelling punch, we talk of chasing. The detail of a dagger sheath shows a particularly successful example of this technique.

4) The use of bottom swages: Ill. 132

To obtain simultaneously shapes and patterns, silverplate, over which an easily malleable material (mostly sheet lead) is placed to reduce the chances of deformation, is driven into a matrix or bottom swage with hammer blows. Our illustration shows the front and back of typical pendants to a piece of Turkmen jewellery.

5) Open work:

Ills. 133, 134

To obtain open work ornaments, tinplate was sawn through, cut out, or broken through with hammer and chisel. The last method was mostly used in Turkestan. Our detail of a Turkmen ornamental disk (a) and an Uzbek belt (b) is meant to show the widely different effects that can be achieved with this method. The character of open work can also be obtained by open casting, but this technique played hardly any part in Turkestan.

6) Cut steel work:

Ill. 135

Technologically speaking, there is no difference between engraving and cut steel work. We speak of engraving when the chip removing technique is applied to forming a pattern in lines. If a flat pattern is formed using the same technique, as is frequent in weapons – in our case the blade of a Turkmen dagger – we speak of cut steel work. (The name is somewhat incorrectly applied to open work as well.)

7) File décor: Ill. 136

Chip removing patterns can also be formed at the edge of a piece with the help of a file. Our detail shows the edge of a Turkmen fire lighter.

8) Damascening: Ill. 137

A hard base metal – mostly iron – is ornamented with inlays or overlays of a softer decorative metal (gold, silver or copper). The more important technique in Turkestan is overlay. The base metal is prepared by chisel blows and pieces of decorative metal cut to the required shape are hammered on to it. This detail of the blade of an urban dagger shows places where the damascening has disappeared and the prepared background is clearly visible.

9) Fire gilding: Ill. 138

Fire gilding is a technique using very little metal. Gold dust is mixed with quicksilver. This mixture, the amalgam, is transferred to the piece. When heated the quicksilver evaporates and the gold fuses with the background. After that the gilding can be given a final polish (cf. p. 104)

10) Enamelling:

Ills. 139, 140

Enamelling is the fusing of glass coloured by metal oxide on to a metal ground. If the glass is burnt into channels cut in the metal ground, we speak of *émail champlevé* (a); if cells are formed by soldering thin metal strips on to the ground metal and molten glass is poured into them, we speak of *émail cloisonné* (b). As the details in our photos show, both techniques appear side by side in Bukhara.

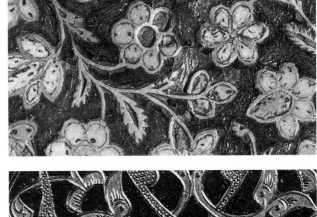

11) Nielloing:

Ill. 141

The ground for nielloing is prepared as for *émail champlevé*. Niello is an alloy of silver, copper, lead and sulphur with borax as the liquid medium. The components of the alloy are washed, pounded and after they have been introduced into the hollows in the metal ground, smelted by firing. After firing, the blue-black or black niello has to be smoothed out and polished. This detail of a belt clasp is a typical example of Bukhara niello work.

12) Wax inlays: Ill. 142

An effect similar to enamelling or nielloing can be obtained with much less expense by introducing sealing-wax into hollows in the metal ground. The technique is common in North India and presumably came from there to Bukhara where it is supposed to have spread as a decorative element on metal vessels, but was also used on jewellery such as our belt fastening.

13) Filigree: Ill. 143

Filigree is one of the techniques of appliqué. Appliqué is a general term for the fusing of wires, sheet metal, ornamental stones, etc., on to the piece. Fine wires are bent into patterns and soldered on to the piece – in this case a Khiva amulet. If wires are soldered to one another and not applied to a piece, we speak of à jour filigree. This technique is not often found in Turkestan.

14) 'Gallery wire': Ill. 144

The production of gallery wire is a variation of filigree work. The wire, in the desired form, is wound round rows of nails on a board, then removed and soldered to the piece. 'Gallery wire' is an important decorative element of Turkestan jewellery. Comparison of the extremely fine wire of a Teke pendant with the coarse wire of a north Afghan (Saryq?) piece shows the very different effects that can be obtained, depending on the delicacy of the work.

15) Turquoise inlay works:

Ill. 145

These were a speciality of Bukhara craftsmen. Narrow strips of silver plate were soldered to the piece in a honeycomb pattern. The honeycombs were partially filled with a resinous mass into which the turquoises were pressed. The technique was used on horse adornments or – as in our example – on small jewellery chests.

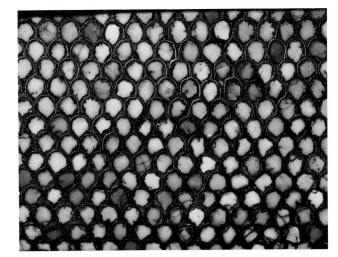

16) Application of sheet metal:

Ill. 146

The soldering of sheet metal beaten in matrices is primarily a technique characteristic of Yomut jewellery. Gilded rhomboid sheets were soldered to a neck ornament.

17) Settings:

Ill. 147

The usuall setting of Turkestan jewellery is the box setting. It is formed of strips of sheet metal. 'The stone rests on the base plate of the setting and is held by the vertical sides of the box, the upper edges of which are pressed down over the stone.' (Brepohl 1962, after Janata 1981). A graphic example is offered by the setting of a cornelian on a heart-shaped Turkmen decorative dorsal plate from Northern Afghanistan.

Examples of Textile Techniques

Next to the metal work, the excellent textile products undoubtedly represent the most important examples of Turkestan craftsmanship, together with the home weaving practised by the women. A survey of only the most typical and technologically interesting textile products from the region would require a comprehensive publication. We have already mentioned the importance which both everyday textiles and decorative wear assume in rural and urban households, and the wealth of textile techniques observed in costume. A series of technical works about carpets have dealt intensively with the technology of knotted products and flat-weaving (kelims). These publications are well known and easily accessible to anyone with a special interest in the subject. Ikat production, which has been thoroughly investigated by A. Bühler, has been discussed in an earlier section. So the following exposition will concentrate on the most neglected area, that of embroidery. In books on the subject to date, the indigenous (Uzbek, Tadzhik or Turkmen) names of the stitches are mainly given and they are meaningless for a correct technological classification of the works. Consequently we shall illustrate the most important embroidery stitches and name them after the usual standard works. Our selection of illustrations is meant to show how quite a broad spectrum of differentiated patterns is achieved with relatively few stitches. The last part of the chapter explains some of the so far lesser known techniques in this area and an example of relief knotting.

Turkmen embroideries

1. Detail of a women's coat (chyrpy) of the Teke Turkmen. Silk on cotton executed in a very tight variation of chain stitch.

Ill. 149 Chain stitch variation

2. Detail of the embroidered turn-up of a woman's trousers, silk on cotton, Ersari Turkmen, northern Afghanistan. The chain stitch variation as in 1. was used for surface embroidery. The outlines of the central ornament composed of four flowers were emphasised by stem stitches in black silk.

Ill. 150 Stem stitch

3. Detail of a rear pigtail ornament of a northern Afghan Turkmen group (Ersari?). Silk on cotton with silver appliqué. Loose embroidery in comparatively large satin-stitches. Ornamental yurt bands embroidered in the same technique are more common.

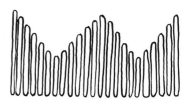

Ill. 151 Satin stitch

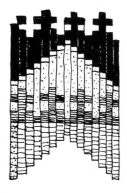

Ill. 148   Embroidery pattern of a man's cap from Tashkurgan

144

Uzbek embroideries and other urban embroideries

4. Detail of a triangular ornamental band of the Lakai Uzbek. Silk on cotton, cross stitch. Two styles of embroidery are attributed to the Lakai. Embroideries done in cross-stitch are always made to cover the whole surface and have geometric ornaments.

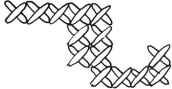

Ill. 152 Cross stitch

5. Detail of a Lakai Uzbek mirror case. Silk on wool executed in a loose chain-stitch variation. This stitch was used in Lakai embroideries which did not cover the background fabric, but consisted of large poster-like floral curvilinear or theriomorphic ornaments on a red or more rarely black ground.

6. Detail of a man's cap, silk on wool, executed in half-cross stitch.

Ill. 153 Half-cross stitch

7. Detail of a man's cap, Tashkurgan, silk on cotton in whipped stem stitch. Ornamentation in whipped stem stitch is the most widespread technique for men's caps in northern Afghanistan.

Ill. 154 Whipped stem stitch

8. Detail of a rear pigtail ornament, silk on cotton. The style reminiscent of a susani, allows us to conclude on an origin in the environs of Bukhara. Even after an intensive examination of the piece one cannot say with certainty whether it is embroidery in chain stitch or tambour work.

9. Section of a cloth food cover, silk on cotton, possibly the work of Bukhara Jews. The embroidery, which almost covers the surface was done in pulled thread stitch with diagonal overcast stitches.

Ill. 155 Overcast stitch

10. Section of a frontlet, metal threads on a velvet ground. A technique of relief embroidery is used here. Underlying shapes (in our case, of card) are stitched over. The gold braid framing the relief was applied by the inlay technique.

Other textile techniques

11. Section of veiling used by Turkmen, cotton. The décor of the fabric, made in an urban manufactory, is pierced and sewn.

12. Section of a large handprinted cotton cloth (table-cloth, niche curtain or bedspread). We have no definite indications saying in which Turkestan towns handprinted fabrics were produced. In the period from which most travel books come, indigenous printed fabrics seem to have been already supplanted by Russian imports. The piece, made of narrow coarse handwoven strips sewn together, probably originated before 1880.

13. Section of a Turkmen veil, silk. Pattern produced as printed batik.

14. Section of a large tent band, wool, Teke Turkmen (cf. Ill. 34). Knotted relief work in flat-weave.

Technological details from:

Boser. R. and Müller, J. 1969: *Stickerei. Systematik der Stichformen.* Museum für Völkerkunde, Basel (Bale).

Bühler-Oppenheim, K. and others, 1948: *Die Textilsammlung Fritz Ilké-Huber im Museum für Völkerkunde und Schweizerisches Museum für Völkerkunde, Basel. (Grundlagen der gesamten textilen Technik.)* Zürich.

Dillmont, Thérèse de, undated: *Encyklopaedie der Weiblichen Handarbeiten.* Bibliothek. D. M. C. Mühlhausen.

Rol, N., 1980: *Kleines Lexikon der Stickerei, Stiche und Techniken.* Hanover.

Ill. 156   Textile techniques

1.   Detail of Turkmen woman's coat

4.   Detail of a Lakai Uzbek
     decorative band

2.   Detail of the turn-up of a
     Turkmen woman's trousers

5.   Detail of a Lakai Uzbek
     mirror case

3.   Detail of a Turkmen woman's head adornment

6. and 7.   Detail of a man's cap

11. Section of a Turkmen veil

8. Detail of a rear pigtail
   pattern in susani style

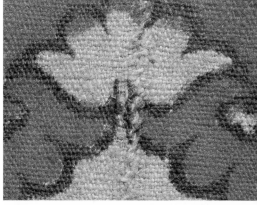

12. Section of a printed cover

9. Section of a food cover,
   Bukhara?

*13. Section of a Turkmen veil,
   using the batik technique*

10. Section of a frontlet,
    Bukhara

*14. Section of Turkmen tent band
    with relief knotting*

The Basic Design Principles of Turkestan Popular Art

Ornaments – Symbols; Shapes – Colours

Turkestan popular art originated in an area with a very ancient Islamic tradition. Consequently this popular art is *inter alia* a legitimate child of Islamic art. Besides the use of writing – it plays a very minor role in popular art – Islamic art has always been characterised as an ornamental art.*) Yet ornaments have some importance in certain periods of European art (e. g. Art Nouveau). But in Europe they ultimately remain decorative accessories which may or may not have symbolic significance. H. Schneider has correctly described the quite different function of Islamic ornament: 'Islamic ornament is something entirely different. It is based on comparatively few forms, but turns these into an infinity of variations. It is shallow and the spatial interweaving of the forms is limited to the least possible depth. The highly abstract and non-natural forms include the intermediate space. The sequence of their endless repetition is executed with consistent austerity. This endless unfolding is the basic principle of Islamic decorative art. . .' European ornament, on the other hand, is often planned for only a limited surface. A difference of content corresponds to this formal difference. The 'endless unfolding' of arabesques – the non-natural forked leaf runner (Ill. 158) which undoubtedly represents the best-known Islamic ornamental motif – or of plaited star systems symbolises the infiniteness of God. Runner motifs have frequently undergone considerable transformations in the development of Islamic art often under influences from outside the Islamic cultural area. The fillings of triangles and wedges with runner motifs were also subject to change. A comparison of the forms occurring in urban cultural spheres and among the nomads

shows that the ornamentation, e. g. Teke decoration, is clearly closer to early Islamic ornamentation than the urban metal works, which were much more exposed to changes in fashion.

When presenting the material inventory of Turkmen and urban cultures, it has always been necessary to examine ornamentation and individual motifs as well. This has shown that forms and ornaments, mainly of material of urban provenance, are not solely of Islamic origin nor the result of influence by the neighbouring Chinese and Indian cultures in historical times (from c. the 8th century B. C.). The essential roots of the ornamentation and symbolism of the peoples of Turkestan are to be sought in ancient oriental cultural traditions, which become evident from the end of the 4th to the beginning of the 3rd millennium; other roots were in the spiritual world of the nomadic steppe peoples who before their conversion to Islam were followers of natural religions, with partially shamanistic ideas. This statement can only be illustrated here by a few selected examples. Before we start with these individual examples, an aspect must be tackled that is even more important in our opinion. A comparison of handicraft products made by men, for example Turkmen jewellery, with the work of Turkmen women (embroidery) and products of home industry (knotted ware) shows that two completely different ornamental traditions persist in the repertory of a group. In Ill. 161, for example, which shows the ornamentation of a Teke amulet holder, it is obvious that it corresponds in its overall structure to the ornamentation of a 'classical Islamic' urban carpet, a field of tiles or the décor of a piece of stucco work. Equally obvious is the Islamic origin of the runners reproduced from pieces of jewellery when they are

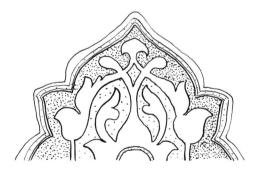

Ill. 157 Contour filling made up of runners, left from a Turkmen belt fastening, right from a cosmetic flask from Bukhara

---

*) The author has attempted to describe the origins of Islamic art and ornamentation in more detail elsewhere (Kalter, 1982).

148

Ill. 158 *Forked leaf runner, left from a Ghasnevid stone relief, (12th c.), right from a piece of Teke jewellery (cf. Ill. 123 left)*

Ill. 159 *Highly stylised runners, left from a Ghasnevid stone relief, right from a piece of Teke jewellery*

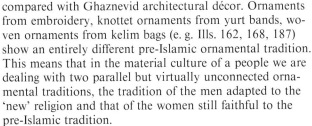

Ill. 160 *Interwoven runner from a piece of Teke jewellery*

compared with Ghaznevid architectural décor. Ornaments from embroidery, knottet ornaments from yurt bands, woven ornaments from kelim bags (e. g. Ills. 162, 168, 187) show an entirely different pre-Islamic ornamental tradition. This means that in the material culture of a people we are dealing with two parallel but virtually unconnected ornamental traditions, the tradition of the men adapted to the 'new' religion and that of the women still faithful to the pre-Islamic tradition.

The special situation of women in the Islamic world, which is more strictly divided into a male and female world than in any other culture, certainly encouraged this development. But to a less striking degree this statement surely applies to every popular culture. Women are traditionally the more conservative, preservative element in a society. These statements are not intended to imply that Islamic conceptions left the field of female artistic activity completely unchanged. Many authors who have dealt with questions of carpet ornamentation point out that animal representations on nomad carpets, originally much commoner, were often abstracted to the point of unrecognisability or transformed into floral patterns. Bird representations on göls – octagonal primary ornaments of Turkmen knotted carpets, which are supposed to have served as tribal emblems – have been shown, for example, on the göls of Salor and Saryk Turkmen. According to medieval Islamic sources (Rashid ed-Din) birds of prey in particular are supposed to have been the totemic animals of Turkmen tribes. Representations of horned animals sometimes occur in Teke knotted products. The most striking animal representations on Turkmen knotted ware are found on the so-called tauk nuska göl of the Arabatchi (Moschkova). Even the names of many ornaments listed by Moschkova are reminiscent of animal tracks, parts of animals, etc. Often only characteristic parts were represented instead of the whole animal.

Ill. 161 *Ornamental field of a Teke amulet holder. The arrangement is like that of a 'classical' carpet*

Ill. 162   Rams' horn ornament from a Lakai embroidery

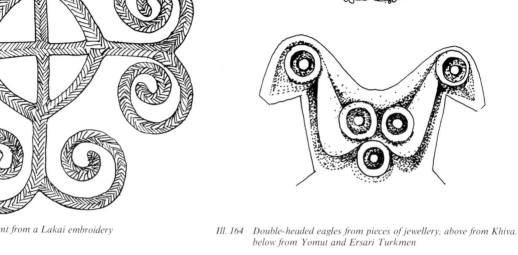

Ill. 164   Double-headed eagles from pieces of jewellery, above from Khiva, below from Yomut and Ersari Turkmen

Ill. 163   Rams' horn ornament from a cap, Tashkurgan

Some of the best known are rams' horns, which among both Uzbeks and Turkmen can be combined into complicated ornamental structures on textile materials. They are connected with ideas of power. In the case of birds, too, parts can stand for the whole: the wings, the head or more frequently a double head. Duplication may also signify the duplication of magical protection. I have already mentioned that in the case of these double-headed birds we should think of the double-headed eagle, an ancient Central Asian symbol of sovereignty. These double-headed eagles can be most clearly observed as the upper termination of Turkmen and urban pieces of jewellery (Ills. 164, 165, 166). The eyes

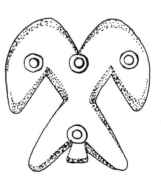

Ill. 165   Lakai embroidery, silk on cotton. Square cloths of this kind were used for covering breadbaskets, but also as wall ornaments. Length: 62 cm; width: 59 cm

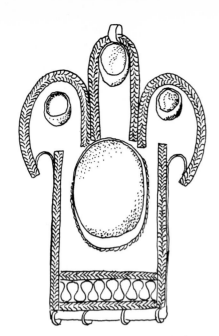

Ill. 166   Double-headed eagle from an Ersari chain diadem

are mostly emphasised by inlays of glass or stones. Lastly, H. Baranski has referred to the constant danger of confusion which goes with *pars pro toto* representations, such as birds' wings and rams' horns. He traces this danger to the abbreviated representation that meets the need of textile techniques. We have already seen that this danger of confusion or the impossibility of deciding in individual cases whether horn or bird representations are concerned applies even more to jewellery. As the subject is still being heatedly discussed, we repeat a brief summary of our own opinion. Ill. 85 a, left, reproduces rams' horns, while Ill. 99 shows rams' heads, but the forms on the right of 85 a and 99 could equally well be representations of birds. Trefoil motifs as shown in Ill. 167 are often interpreted as abstracted bird's claws by Russian colleagues. It is interesting that these zoomorphic ornaments from the field of ancient cul-

Ill. 167   Trefoil motif from a piece of Teke jewellery

tural 'female ornamentation' often appear in the centre of textile products and form patterns. In jewellery made by men they are forced to the edge and often seem alien beside Islamic surface ornamentation; they are frequently more se-

verely abstracted than in textiles. This juxtaposition of male and female ornamental traditions is also found in Uzbek material. Embroideries by rural Uzbek women show a close affinity in their motifs to those of their Turkmen neighbours. Illustration 168 shows a highly abstract representation of an eagle from a small Lakai bag. The fact that the Islamisation of the cities was much more protracted, as has been frequently mentioned, is also proved in our opin-

Ill. 168   Representation of an eagle from an embroidered Lakai bag

ion by urban embroidery. Here we cannot establish anything about a specifically female sphere of ornamentation. The embroideries are based on the Islamic ornamental traditions current at the time they were made. We have referred to the influence of neighbouring regions. Occasional bird representations appearing on susanis, mostly to be identified as cocks, are the last reminiscence of pre-Islamic pictorial traditions – the cock is of course one of the ancient animal symbols of the sun – which are not integrated into the ornamental system, but have an alien effect.

The products of urban carpenters (Ill. 44) and metal workers also occasionally exhibit, compared with nomadic material, very naturalistic bird representations which, as already happens in Ghaznevid and Seljuk works, are incorporated into runner work. To prove the astonishing persistence of such motifs, we show a drawing (169) from a 12th-c. Ghaznevid metal vessel – it could be a green magpie, often represented in miniatures too – and a second drawing from a samovar made in Bukhara, presumably at the beginning of the 20th c. In view of the often mentioned hostility to pictorial art of orthodox Islam, the naturalism of the representation may be surprising in pieces coming from strongholds of Islamic Sunnite culture. Consequently we should remember that miniature painting is also an art originating in the urban sphere that was equally in demand in Shiite

and Sunnite courts. Turkestan in particular was one of the great centres of miniature painting in the late Middle Ages.

We should like to mention the dragon's head as a final interesting zoomorphic motif. We find it from Timurid times as the termination of vessel handles and according to Melikian-Chirvani (1973) it was supposed to protect the contents of the vessel from contamination, but it also occurs on Yomut earrings, in which case it probably had significance as an amulet (Ill. 170).

In the floral décor of textile products made by Turk-

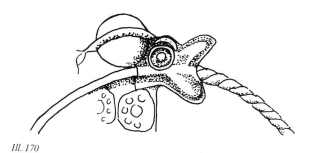

Ill. 170

men women, more recent pieces also exhibit an increasing tendency towards abstraction. But it does not go nearly so far, because floral motifs are in no way subject to religiously motivated rejection. Undoubtedly the most striking motif on Turkmen embroidery (it appears on all other textile products, too, but not on jewellery) is the tree of life. Representations of the tree of life on whose tip sits a bird as symbol of sovereignty are already common in Central Asia at the beginning of the third millennium BC (Janata 1981). In Turkestan they coincide with shamanistic ideas of Altai peoples about the world's pillars and axis (often looked on

Ill. 171

Following two pages

Ill. 172 Prayer carpet, Beshir (Turkmen), dated 1311 Hegira – 1893 AD, 150 by 86 cm

Ill. 173 Above: Transport- and storage bag, kelim, décor on the front side in the sumak technique, Uzbek. Below: double bag used on horses and asses as saddlebags, kelim with knotted strips, Turkmen, north Afghanistan. Measurements: 77 by 51 cm, opened out, 113 by 45 cm

153

*Ill. 174 Tree of life motifs, left from a Turkmen woman's coat, above right
from an ikat cover, below from a man's cap*

as a tree on whose top and branches birds sit), which support the many-layered vaults of heaven. (Baranski, after Holmberg). Trees of life may be wholly floral (174) or reduced to the purely schematic (187). The trefoils on the ends of the branches of these examples could possibly be interpreted as birds' claws. Illustration 11 shows a wholly schematic example, the upper termination of which we should interpret as rams' horns, if we did not know that it must be an eagle. They appear on yurt bands as vigorous trees of life, the tips of whose boughs could represent birds. Even a reduction to three leaves and blossoms may still represent the tree of life. This reduction frequently occurs in Turkmen knotted work (cf. the secondary ornaments on the lower border of the choval, Ill. 6) and is especially common in urban material. Illustration 174, bottom right, shows such a motif on an embroidered Bukhara cap. In the urban cultural province we find not only schematic, but also very clear tree of life motifs, which were made by highly specialised craftsmen. Does that not contradict our thesis of male (Islamic) and female (pre-Islamic) ornamental spheres? We do not think so if Bühler and Janata are correct in saying that ikats were made in Turkestan as early as the 8th c. AD, i. e. at a time when the Islamisation of the area was still in its infancy. Janata (1981) has referred to the complex of fertility concepts connected with the tree of life. This is most strikingly depicted in an example of an ikat with the tree of life in the form of a cypress (Ill. 174, above right) – a form which could have been adopted from the Zoroastrian religion of pre-Islamic Iran. From it grow pomegranates which are looked on as a fertility symbol throughout the East (because of their many seeds). The disk above the cypress, but not attached to it, could be interpreted as a symbol of the sun.

Flower representations: the flower most widely depicted on Turkmen embroidery is the tulip, which also plays a large part in Iranian and Osman Turkish art. The interpretation of three-leaved shapes as tulips, as they already appear on 12th-c. Ghaznevid marble reliefs and in a very similar form on Ersari and Teke jewellery (Ill. 12), seems rather rash, but not impossible when we remember how longingly the nomad awaits the first rain which makes the steppe blossom, the first flowers being tulips (and other members of the onion family). In addition, Compositae and orchid shapes are common. Moschkova interprets this standard motif on Ersari knotted work as 'flying birds'. This interpretation is unconvincing in both the representation of individual and serial motifs.

The floral motifs of urban embroidery (cf. p. 69 and Ill. 57) are mostly non-naturalistic. The commonest floral motif on urban metal-work is the stylised lotus blossom which appears in medallions (Ill. 20) or may form runners (Ill. 21). Both motifs, in this or similar form, can be identified in the Turkestan region and in neighbouring Iran, since

Timurid times. Illustration 20 shows a single blossom from a Timurid metal work (reproduction after a photograph in Melikian-Chirvani 1982). Illustration 21 was drawn after a reputedly Kokand teapot. Unlike Westphal-Hellbusch, we see their models in Indian rather than in Chinese lotus blossom forms.

Here we shall refer only briefly to another group of motifs, the representation of amulets or amulet-like (?) pieces of jewellery and everyday objects. They occur overwhelmingly in textile material. The best known are knotted symbols of triangular amulet holders as secondary ornaments on carpets. Illustration 175 shows an example from an embroidered Tashqurgan man's cap. Illustrations 176 and 177 were taken from a dark-blue Turkmen woman's coat (chyrpy). In one case, it is clearly an amulet topped by rams' horns that is shown, in the other an ear or false ear ornament. We were struck by such representations falling outside the usual floral patterns on the dark-blue chyrpys

Ill. 175

often preferred by younger women. It would be tempting to connect them with fertility representations, but they may simply symbolise the bride's wealth. Similar conceptions may lie behind representations of pieces of jewellery cut from silver plate in the shape of a rosewater flask on frontlets embroidered in the Lakai style. (At the opposite end of the Islamic world, in north-west Morocco, rosewater flasks on painted bridal chests were also explained to me as symbols of wealth, well-being and fertility.) The rural embroi-

Ill. 176

157

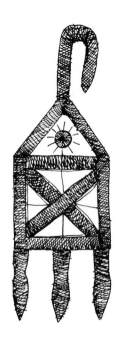

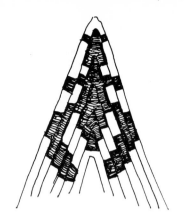

numbers 3, 4, 5, 7, 9 and 12 that seem to have a specific significance. We have mentioned the example of 5 in another place (p. 134). The number 4 could be connected with the idea of the four points of the compass or the four elements (earth, air, fire and water). The data about colours are even more copious. The unmistakable preference of the Turkmen for the colour red is always mentioned and underlined by a Yomut woman's lullaby. 'Sleep, sleep, my

dery of Uzbek groups is rich in motifs that are hard or impossible to interpret. Illustrations 179 and 180 may be representations of insects; 181 reminds us of a solar wheel. Our drawing 182 from a Lakai embroidery, showing the so-

called heart-cum-ram's horn or kasa kalkan motif, provides a final example of the difficulty in interpreting combined ornamentation.

The references in the literature to numeral symbolism are of such a general nature that it seems pointless to go into them in detail. Among the Turkmen, it is mainly the

Ill. 181

Ill. 182

darling. When journeying, thou shalt ride a red camel, at thy marriage, thou shalt wear a red dress, sleep, sleep my dearest.'

Red is also the outstanding colour for urban embroidery and ikat fabrics, but is not nearly as dominant as among the Turkmen. Blue has an apotropaic significance against the evil eye.

We have not tried, even if it had been possible, to mention even the most important forms, symbols and ornaments. We have only tried to give a brief survey of this wide field, because we are convinced that preoccupation with it may offer the key to an understanding of Turkestan popular art and so of an important aspect of Turkestan culture. One of the great connoisseurs of carpet ornamentation, D. Wegner, has accurately described the difficulty of this undertaking: 'It is easy to see that such a cryptic symbolism from interwoven and often obscure traditions stubbornly resists all attempts at an interpretation using our own criteria. To all appearances interpretations too easily overlook the real significance of a motif. Every such error only increases our alienation from the very men whom we ought to understand better if we wish to comprehend Central Asia.'

Ill. 183   Teke pendant in the shape of a samovar

159

Reflections on the Ornamentation of Central Asian Carpets

(Walter Böhning)

'In the eastern region, different custons are assciated with various design. On Solor, not the design temselves but the arrangement of them was the property of an individual clan.'

This quotation refers to woven material on the island of Solor, one of the Sunda Isles, east of Flores. It continues: 'A person who wore a textile belonging to another group would be considered a 'thief'.' (M. Gittinger, *Splendid Symbols, Textile and Tradition in Indonesia.* The Textile Museum, Washington, D. C. 1979, p. 169. A source from 1932 is quoted (E. Vatter, *Ata Kivan,* Leipzig 1932) which establishes this special attitude to textile patterns and their arrangement as the sign of belonging to a certain clan, even if this system is no longer preserved and perhaps would not even be mentioned in reply to questions by a presentday visitor. The example shows that systems of social and ethnic characteristics can lose their meaning and lapse into oblivion in a comparatively short time. Even if the characteristics – in this case woven fabrics – are preserved or produced in the traditional form, the resultant patterns can only be listed systematically.

That is the unsatisfactory situation in which we find ourselves with regard to the rich treasure of patterns to be observed on the carpets and knotted ware of Central Asia. When studying the carpet patterns of Central Asia, one would expect that the accounts of early travellers and especially Russian scholars, would contain similar facts about the significance and manner of their use. Unfortunately, the older texts, apart from the occasional mention of carpets and some details of their manufacture and use, contain no utilizable reference to their pattern or even their contents. Likewise, nothing is said about the fact that certain ornaments were used not only as decorative elements, but also as emblems of groups or tribes.

One hundred years ago, a book entitled *L'Art de l'Asie centrale* by N. Simakoff was published in what was then St Petersburg. Turkmen carpets were illustrated in it for the first time. Simakoff traced the fantastic figures in the patterns to the poisonous insects living in the steppes, the scorpions and tarantulas, which are a great plague to the inhabitants. Simultaneously carpet knotting in Central Asia underwent a frightening decline. In many districts, the times when the female craftswomen worked only to supply their own needs were past, and the important centres of knotting were producing hastily for commercial interests, using the poor quality aniline dyes of the period and processing inferior qualities of wool, in order to produce the necessary

quantities for export. They were sold not only to Russia and Western Europe, but also reached America. A book which attempted to classify Turkmen carpets of the different tribes for the first time appeared there in 1900 (J. K. Mumford, *Oriental Rugs,* New York 1900). This attempt was based on a knowledge of the trade, which even then was complaining about an enormous rise in prices with a simultaneous loss of quality, and recommended that the decline should be counteracted by government aid. An anonymous report in the periodical *Export,* the organ of the Zentralverein für Handelsgeographie (no 7, p. 94, Berlin 1901) must be quoted at somewhat greater length as it summarises the situation at the turn of the century brilliantly and also describes the conditions under which the carpets of this region, now looked on as antiques, originated.

'The Carpet Industry in Central Asia

Originally the carpets were made simply to meet the needs of the indigenous population: nomadic Turkmen, Bukharans and Sariks took pleasure in the variegated carpets that satisfied their highly developed sense of colour and only allowed their wives to work for the decoration of their houses or tents. Only later, in recent times, has the carpet turned into a much sought-after article of trade on the world market, and that simultaneously started the decline of the carpet industry.

It seldom happens that European traders make the very costly and arduous journey to Merv, Bukhara and Teheran; on the other hand, many representatives of the large carpet firms from Vienna, Paris, Berlin, Hamburg, New York and other cities come annually to Tiflis, where they find the widest selection of carpets of different kinds and make purchases for hundreds of thousands of roubles.

Beginning three or four years ago, prices have risen on an average by 25 to 35 per cent, and for certain types, such as old Sumak, Tekins and similar kinds, by as much as 50 to 60 per cent. This, of course, applies to old carpets, as they are the only ones that are in such brisk demand.

This enormous increase in the price of old carpets is attributable not so much to the increasing demand, but rather to the circumstance that the old carpets become rarer and rarer and, because modern manufacture is much inferior, they are not replaced by similar new ones. Tekins, which were obtainable two or three years ago for 60 to 80 roubles, today cost 120 to 150 roubles and often cannot be found even at those prices. Old Yamut, Merv, Pendeh, Khiva and Kisel Ajak carpets are also becoming increasingly rare.

Things have changed greatly since the extension of the railway line. The old carpets are and were bought in

160

large quantities and, seduced by the high prices, makers have turned to mass production; manufacture has to be fast and large-scale. In particular less care was taken in the production of colours; the traditional deep, lasting, vegetable dyes were replaced by the much cheaper but much shorter lived, harsh, aniline dyes and in the process the whole carpet industry took on a different character. Makers were far more careless with the knotting and the product was not only much inferior in colour and design, but also could not be compared in delicacy and durability with the products of the old technique.

It is true that the workers mostly execute their drawings from memory, but previously their eye was trained by the constant presence of classical models, which will soon no longer be the case. Consequently the recommendation was recently made that the state should buy all the extant old genuinely classically beautiful carpets, which would be widely distributed in coloured reproductions.'

Such collections of patterns were formed by government representatives on their official journeys. For example, between 1896 and 1901 A. A. Bogoljubov collected mainly Turkmen carpets, which he published in a magnificently produced album in 1908 (*Les Tapis de l'Asie centrale,* St Petersburg, Part I 1908, Part II 1909.) This album introduced Central Asian carpets to the interested public of Western Europe, as did his proposal to divide Turkmen carpets into three groups, the Salor, Yomut and Ersari carpets, with which he associated yet other groups. In addition, he viewed Kirgiz, Uzbek and Arab carpets as a separate group. By and large, all divisions since then follow his proposals. He looked on the carpets as ethnohistorical documents and tried to classify the patterns by formal criteria. At the same time, however, he expressed the hope that one day, by careful study and with the help of a second Champollion, we might be in a position to recognise as hieroglyphs what we still regard as ornaments. Then we should be able to read a tent band pattern in the way Egyptologists read inscriptions on their monuments. Since then, this desire to interpret individual patterns by content and evidence has dominated the discussion of Central Asian ornamentation and ranges from explaining it as purely ornamental and without intrinsic meaning to interpretation as representations of the real world, especially the environment of the inhabitants of Central Asia. The latter view largely resulted from the names of the patterns which became known in the course of research and contained many such indications, but are not the same among all peoples.

The first expedition using ethnographic methods when researching Central Asian knotted carpets started in 1929. Bogoljubov had directed attention to the main carpet patterns, the göls, which he considered as characteristic of the different tribal traditions. 1946 saw the appearance of an article on this subject by V. G. Moschkova, which was translated into German two years later: 'Göls auf turkmenischen Teppichen.' (Transl. by Sepp Kuntschik; in *Archiv für Völkerkunde,* Vol III, pp, 24–43, Vienna 1948.) Although the authoress knew all the Russian publications on the subject and had spent seventeen years analysing the Central Asian carpets in museum collections and on expeditions, she started with a very cautious definition of the concept göl: 'The göl is the pattern peculiar to a specific tribe on the central field of a Turkmen carpet. In fact, there is no satisfactory translation or explanation of the word 'göl'. In the absence of a satisfactory interpretation, it is best to accept the 'göl' as the pattern, ornament and emblem belonging to a tribe and try to explain it on the road to solving the forms it represents. The stability of the 'göls' can be explained by the fact that they reflect certain tribal and family emblems, the representation of which was once presumably subject to strict rules and later changed into a permanent tradition.'

Moschkova herself has travelled the road to solving the forms the göls represent and, after she believed she had found representations of birds (or birds and other animals) on at least four tribal göls from quite different Turkmen tribes, came to the conclusion that 'tribal göls (had) in their original representation some compositions, which included birds and other animals (perhaps plants as well) in their repertory, the surviving forms of which we find in the tribal göls of contemporary Turkmen with more or less realistic features.' The four göls with animal representations were the Teke göl, the Saryk göl, the ertmen of the Chaudor and the tauk nuska of the Arabachi.

In addition, she differentiated between living and dead göls, depending on whether they were still regarded as tribal signs by female knotmakers or were abandoned and simply considered as decorative shapes. She traced the representations of birds as tribal Turkmen göls to totemic animals mentioned in a 14th-c. source (Rashid-ad-Din: *Jamiat-Tawarich*). Twenty years later A. N. Pirkulieva postulated a quite different origin of the tribal göl in her study of 'Teppichweberei der Turkmenen aus dem Tal des mittleren Amu Darya' (Moscow 1966, German in: *Turkmenenforschung* Vol IV, Hamburg 1981, p. 52): 'Undoubtedly this motif is based on the representation of a single plant in which the forms gradually simplify, alter and acquire the outline of a rosette. This is conclusive proof that the tribes named consider themselves to be the bearers of a common culture who had settled in the period of their common historical evolution in the 11th to the 17th century in the extensive territory of the Balkhan, Sarykamish and Usboi.'

With the exception of the Saryk, she refers to the tribes of the Ersari, Teke, Salor and Yomut, i. e. all important producers of carpets with tribal göls.

The debate about tribal göls has not ended and this exposition is far from containing all contributions on the sub-

Ill. 184   Knotted frame of a yurt door, Yomut, 160 by 130 cm

*Ill. 185   Above: knotted torba, Ersari, 155 by 92 cm. Below: large knotted
bag (choval), Yomut, 128 by 75 cm*

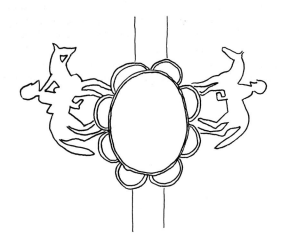

Ill. 186   Representation of riders on a heart-shaped ornamental Teke plate

Independently of the ornamentation considered as peculiar to a tribe, Central Asian knotted ware can be divided into three main groups:

1.) Carpets with tribal göls as the main motif on a central field. The latter may be executed alone or together with one or more additional patterns in straight or staggered rows. The central field is enclosed by a braid frame, which generally consists of a wide border, the main border, which is accompanied on either side by one or more pairs of narrower borders. In many cases an additional braid (elem) is inserted on the narrow side of the carpet.

2.) Carpets with a central field which is divided into vertical, horizontal or diagonal strips or has lattice-like or net-like divisions. The resulting small surfaces are decorated with a succession of one or more patterns.

3.) Knotted products which serve specific purposes and can be patterned according to their format and function. These include door carpets, prayer mats, the various shapes of bags and the other objects in everyday use which are sometimes made by the knotting technique.

ject, but reproduces only a few of the positions adopted by Russian researchers who have had the best opportunity to carry out research among female knotmakers in the field. Just as the significance and function of the tribal göl has not yet been satisfactorily explained, our knowledge of other Central Asian carpet patterns has not grown appreciably, appart from some indications of patterns with a protective function. But we have been given the list of ornaments initially seen as possible. As the result of years of research we have to thank V. G. Moschkova for a large collection of patterns from all the peoples of Central Asia, with detailed descriptions of technical peculiarities, the colours and schemata of the compositions. All the patterns known to her are reproduced in a hundred tables, which puts us in a position today to classify nearly every piece in a tribal tradition. (*Die Teppiche der Völker Mittelasiens im späten XIX. und XX. Jahrhundert.* Tashkent 1970, German by Bernt Rullkötter, 2nd edn. Hamburg 1977), although we cannot be certain that they were really made by members of the actual tribe.

Ill. 187   Tree of life from a Turkmen tent band

When we read in Moschkova that the commercial influence on carpet knotting had already begun in the seventies of the 19th c. and that this craft had already become the most important way of earning a living for some settlements such as, for example, Taimas and Kongur in Mery, Kamashi near Karshi and Beshir and Charchangu near Kerki (Moschkova 1970, p. 32), it becomes clear this development affected not only the quality of the knotting and the dyes, but also the formats and ornamentation, which naturally enough were conditioned more by the taste of the buyer and patron than by traditional conceptions. Consequently, the striking and important main patterns of the carpets changed sooner than the subsidiary patterns or the drawings of the braids.

Older examples were only at the disposal of research, which began comparatively late, in small numbers and recent pieces documented the changes that had occured rather than the original circumstances. For this reason, it can hardly be expected that, progressing beyond the current rough division into tribal traditions, further differentiation or even an interpretation of the patterns will be possible.

Ill. 188 Knotted bicycle saddle cover with the representation of a saddled and bridled horse, north Afghan Turkmen

Bibliography

The bibliography contains only works which are quoted or are of basic importance for the subject. Most works have extensive bibliographies, which can be referred to for more intensive study.

Travel Books

Baer, K. E. v. and Helmersen, G. v., 1839 (1968) (Editors): *Beiträge zur Kenntniss des Russischen Reiches und der angrenzenden Länder Asiens.* Vol. 2. *Helmersen's Nachrichten über Chiwa. Buchara, Chokand und den nordwestlichen Teil des chinesischen Staates.* (New edition, Osnabrück.)

Blocqueville, Henri de Couliboeuf de, 1866: *Quatorze mois de captivité chez les Turcomans 1860–61. In: Le Tour du Monde, premier semestre, p. 225–272.*

Hengstenberg, v., 1899: *Das Orientalische Russland. Reiseeindrücke aus Kiew, der Krim und Mittelasien.* Hamburg.

Karutz, R., 1911: *Unter Kirgisen und Turkmenen.* Leipzig.

Moser, H., 1888: *Durch Zentralasien.* Leipzig.

Schwarz, F. v., 1900: *Turkestan.* Freiburg

Schweinitz, H. H. Graf v., 1910: *Orientalische Wanderungen in Turkestan und im nordöstlichen Persien.* Berlin.

Vambéry, H., 1865: *Reisen in Mittelasien.* Leipzig.

Geography, history and nomadic questions

Barthold, W., 1928: *Turkestan down to the Mongol Invasion.* London.

Brentjes, B., 1976: *Herren der Steppe.* Berlin. 1977: *Mittelasien.* Vienna.

Cahen, C. (editor), 1968: *Der Islam I. Vom Ursprung bis zu den Anfängen des Osmanreiches.* Fischer Weltgeschichte.

Grötzbach, E., 1972: *Kulturgeographischer Wandel in Nordostafghanistan seit dem 19. Jh. Afghanische Studien,* Vol. 4. Meisenheim am Glan. 1979: *Städte und Basare in Afghanistan. Eine stadtgeographische Untersuchung. Beihefte zum Tübinger Atlas des Vorderen Orients.* Wiesbaden.

Hambly, G. (editor), 1966: *Zentralasien. Fischer Weltgeschichte.*

Haussig, H. W., 1966: *Awaren, Shuan-Shuan und Hephthaliten;* in *Handbuch der Orientalistik.* First section, vol. 5, fifth part. Leyden

Jentsch, Ch., 1973: *Das Nomadentum in Afghanistan,* Vol. 9. Meisenheim am Glan.

Jettmar, K., 1966: *Mittelasien und Sibirien in Vortürkischer Zeit. Handbuch der Orientalistik.* First section, Vol. 5, fifth part. Leyden.

Johannsen, U., 1975: *Geschichte und moderne Entwicklung des Nomadismus in Mittelasien;* in *Seminar über das Nomadentum in Zentralasien. Schlußbericht.*

Karger, A. (editor), 1978: *Fischer Länderkunde Sowjetunion.*

Köhalmi, K. U., undated: *Die Periodisierung der Waffengeschichte der Steppennomaden* (manuscript).

Kussmaul, F., 1969: *Das Reiternomadentum als historisches Phänomen;* in *Nomadismus als Entwicklungsproblem.* Bielefeld.

Kraus, W., (editor), 1972: *Afghanistan. Natur, Geschichte und Kultur, Staat, Gesellschaft und Wirtschaft.* Tübingen.

Machatschek, F., 1921: *Landeskunde von Russisch Turkestan.* Stuttgart.

Masson, V. M., 1982: *Das Land der Tausend Städte.* Munich.

Pander, K., 1982: *Sowjetischer Orient. Kunst und Kultur, Geschichte und Gegenwart der Völker Mittelasiens.* Cologne.

Schakir-zade, 1931: *Grundzüge der Nomadenwirtschaft.* Heidelberg thesis. Bruchsal.

Spuhler, B., 1966: *Geschichte Mittelasiens seit dem Auftreten der Türken. Handbuch der Orientalistik.* First section, Vol. 5, first part. Leyden.

Trippett, F., 1978: *Die ersten Reitervölker.* Hamburg.

Wissmann, H. v., 1939: 'Die Klima- und Vegetationsgebiete Eurasiens.' *Zeitschrift der Gesellschaft für Erdkunde zu Berlin,* 1939, Nos 1/2.

1961: Bauer, *Nomade und Stadt im Islamischen Orient* in *Die Welt des Islam und die Gegenwart.* Stuttgart.

Material culture, symbolism and ornamentation

AFJ = Afghanistan Journal

Andrews, P. A., 1971: *The Turcoman of Iran.* Kendal. 1973: 'The White House of Khurasan: The Felt Tents of the Iranian Yomut and Göklen.' in *Iran, 1973. Journal of the British Institute for Persian Studies.*

Azadi, S., 1970: *Turkmenische Teppiche und die ethnographische Bedeutung ihrer Ornamente.* Museum für Völkerkunde, Hamburg.

Baranski, H., 1979: *Tiergestaltige Ornamente im kaukasischen Teppich* in Eder, D.: *Orientteppiche,* Vol. I, *Kaukasische Teppiche.* Munich.

Beresneva, L., 1976: *The Decorative and Applied Art of Turkmenia.* Leningrad.

Besch, F., 1981: *Stickereien aus Mittelasien* in *Susani Stickereien aus Mittelasien,* Bausback catalogue. Mannheim.

Böhning, W., 1982: *Elemente und Gestaltungsprinzipien der Teppichornamente Mittelasiens.* Heidelberg.

Bühler, A., 1972: *Ikat, Batik Plangi,* 3 vols. Basle.

Centlivres, M., 1976: *Jurten aus Zentralasien* in *Seminar über das Nomadentum in Zentralasien.* Berne.

Gentlivres, P., 1972: 'Un bazar d'Asie Centrale. Forme et organisation du bazar de Tashqurghan.' *Beiträge zur Iranistik.* Wiesbaden. 1975: 'Les Usbeks du Qattaghan.' in AFJ, year 2, No 1. Graz.

Dupaigne, B., 1975: *The Ikats of Usbekistan* in *Katalog Usbek.* Basle. 1978: 'Le grand art décoratif des Turkmènes.' in *Objets et Mondes. Revue du Musée de l'Homme.* Vol. 18, fasc. 1–2. Paris.

Faegre, T., 1979: *Tents. Architecture of the Nomads.* London.

Firouz, I. A., 1978: *Silver ornaments of the Turkoman.* Teheran.

Folk Art of Usbekistan, 1979. Tashkent.

Goldmann-Schwartz, 1967/68: *Bokhara. Katalog Israel Museum.* Jerusalem.

Hirschberg, W. and Janata, A., 1966: *Technologie und Ergologie in der Völkerkunde.* Mannheim.

Janata, A., 1981: *Schmuck in Afghanistan.* Graz.

Jettmar, K., 1975: *Die frühen Steppenvölker* (in the series; *Kunst der Welt*). Baden-Baden.

Kalter, J., 1976: *Schmuck aus Nordafrika.* Stuttgart. 1977: *Aus marrokkanischen Bürgerhäusern.* Stuttgart. 1982: 'Der Islamische Orient.' in *Ferne Völker – Frühe Zeiten. Kunstwerke aus dem Linden-Museum Stuttgart.* Recklinghausen.

König, W., 1962: *Die Achal-Teke, Veröffentlichungen des Museums für Völkerkunde Leipzig,* Berlin.

Kusmina, J., 1980: 'Die alten Bodenbauer Afghanistans.' AFJ, year 7, No 4, Graz.

Leix, A., 1974: Turkestan and its textile crafts. The Crosby Press.

May, F., 1961/62: 'Silberschmuck aus der Sammlung Fraschina.' *Jahrbuch des Bernischen Historischen Museums,* XLI and XLII.

Milhofer, S. A., 1968: *Die Teppiche Zentralasiens.* Hannover.

Melikian-Chirvani, A. S., 1973: *Le bronze iranien.* Paris. 1982: *Islamic Metalwork from the Iranian World.* London.

Moschkova, W. G., 1970: *Rugs of the Peoples of Central Asia at the End of the 19th and the Beginning of the 20th Century (Russian).* Tashkent.

Otto-Dorn, K., 1979: *Kunst des Islam.* Revised paperback edition (in the series: *Kunst der Welt*). Baden-Baden.

Pinner, R. and Frances, M., 1980: *Turkoman Studies I.* London

Prokot, I. and J., 1981: *Schmuck aus Zentralasien.* Munich.

Rudolph, H., 1984: *Der Turkmenenschmuck. Sammlung Kurt Gull.* Suttgart, London.

Schienerl, P. W., 1982: 'Die Astralsymbolik im traditionellen Schmuck Afghanistans.' AFJ, year 9, No 2.

Schürmann, U., 1969: *Zentralasiatische Teppiche.* Frankfurt/Main.

Stucki, A., 1978: 'Horses and Women. Some thoughts on the life cycle of Ersari Turkmen women.' AFJ, year 5, No 4, Graz.

Tschjyri, L. A., 1977: *Tadzhik Jewellery (Russian).* Academy of Sciences of the USSR. Institute for Oriental Research.

Wasiljewa, G. P., 1979: *The Costumes of the Peoples of Central Asia (Russian).* Academy of Sciences of the USSR. Institute for Ethnography. Moscow.

Vossen, R., 1980: *Sowjetunion. Völker der Sowjetunion vor und nach der Revolution. Wegweiser zur Völkerkunde.* Hamburgisches Museum für Völkerkunde.

Usbek. The textiles and life of the nomadic and sedentary Usbek tribes of Central Asia. Exhibition catalogue with contributions by B. Dupaigne, M. Frances, Th. Knorr, D. Lindahl and R. Pinner.

Wegner, D. H. G., 1964: 'Nomaden- und Bauernteppiche in Afghanistan.' in *Baessler Archiv,* N. F., Vol. XII.

Textilkunst der Steppen- und Bergvölker Zentralasiens, 1974. Exhibition catalogue of the Basle Textile Museum.

Westphal-Hellbusch, S. and Bruns, J., 1974: *Metallgefäße aus Buchara.* Publications of the Museum für Völkerkunde, NF 29, Berlin.

Westphal-Hellbusch, S. and Soltkahn, G., 1976: *Mützen aus Zentralasien.* Publications of the Museum für Völkerkunde, NF 32, Berlin.

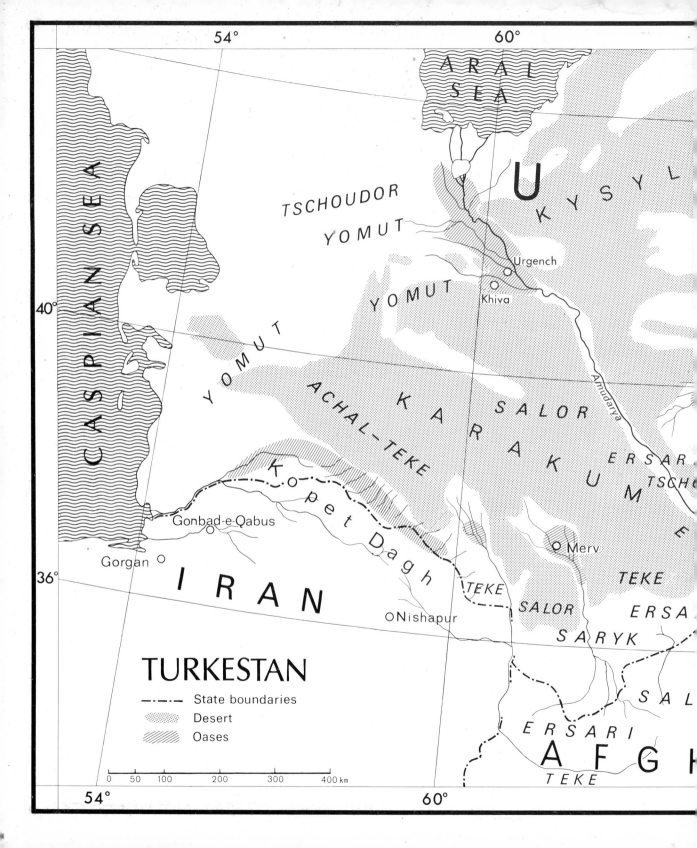

54°   60°

A R A L
S E A

U   K Y S Y L

TSCHOUDOR

YOMUT

Urgench

YOMUT   SALOR

Khiva

C A S P I A N   S E A

40°

YOMUT

Amudarya

YOMUT   K A R A K U M

ACHAL-TEKE   ERSARI

TSCHO

Kopet Dagh

Gonbad-e-Qabus   Merv

TEKE

TEKE

36°   Gorgan   TEKE   ERSA

I R A N   SALOR

Nishapur   SARYK

ERSARI   SAL

TURKESTAN

— ·— ·—   State boundaries

Desert

Oases

AFGH

0 50 100   200   300   400 km

TEKE

54°   60°